THE MARKETING OF INDUSTRIAL AND COMMERCIAL PROPERTY

THE MARKETING OF INDUSTRIAL AND COMMERCIAL PROPERTY

by
EDWARD S. CLEAVELEY
M.Inst.M.

with a Foreword by
PAUL ORCHARD-LISLE
T.D., M.A., F.R.I.C.S.

1984

THE ESTATES GAZETTE LIMITED
151 WARDOUR STREET, LONDON W1V 4BN

FIRST EDITION 1984

ISBN 0 7282 0074 0

©EDWARD S. CLEAVELEY, 1984

Typesetting by Digital Graphics Ltd., 147 Wardour Street, London W1V 3TB
Printed and bound in Great Britain at The Pitman Press, Bath.

To Joan, Helen and James

"Marketing is so basic that it cannot be considered a separate function . . . it is the whole business seen from the point of view of its final result, that is, from the customer's point of view"

PETER DRUCKER
(Author of "Management: Tasks, Responsibilities, Practices."
New York 1973)

Acknowledgements

It would not have been possible to have written this book without the help and advice of many different people who are leaders in their own professional fields. The research that was undertaken depended heavily upon expert opinion and experience that I do not possess. Many are included in the text but to the following who are not, my sincere thanks.

- Tony Biker, Department of Urban Estate Management at The Polytechnic of Wales.
- Karl Wiggins, College of Estate Management, University of Reading.
- Paul Orchard-Lisle, Healey & Baker, London.
- John Craig, Welsh Office, Cardiff.
- Bryn Harries, Berlei (UK) Ltd, Slough.
- Roger Wright, Penarvon PLC, Newport, Gwent.
- David Clowes / Alan Brown, Welsh Development Agency, Cardiff.
- Graham Roberts, Digital (UK) Ltd, Reading.
- Frank Peters, Parrot Corporation, Cwmbran, Gwent.
- John Worthington, Duffy, Ely, Giffone, Worthington, London.
- Philip Bowry, ORC Relocation International Ltd, Bristol.
- Ray Vickers, Comdial Corporation, Maidenhead.
- Dr Charles Sutcliffe, Silicon Valley Management, San Jose, California.
- Dick Deckmann, Deckmann Associates, Pittsburgh, Pennsylvania.
- Bernard Williams, Bernard Williams Associates, London.
- David Stacey, The Bute Partnership, Cardiff.
- Tony Atkin, National Westminster Bank Ltd.
- Joe Clark / Walt Mathews, Mathews & Clark Communications, Palo Alto, California.
- John Traub, Zeropoint, Santa Clara, California.
- George Gray, International Microelectronic Products, San Jose, California.
- Gary Clifford, Coopers & Lybrand Associates, London.

and the senior management of:
- Lion Laboratories, Cardiff.
- Perkin Elmer, Bridgend.
- Pendar Robotics, Bridgewater.
- Speywood Laboratories, Wrexham.
- Raychem, Swindon.
- Videcom, Henley-on-Thames.
- Cifer Systems, Melksham.

FOREWORD

by
Paul Orchard-Lisle, T.D., M.A., F.R.I.C.S.

Ted Cleaveley has produced what is essentially a practical manual on marketing of direct value to those in the real estate market. The thinking and concepts behind the text are clearly those of one who has had to operate in the market as a practising professional.

I believe that we are fortunate to have someone of Mr. Cleaveley's reputation and experience prepared to set forth his views publicly in such a readable manner. It would be unrealistic to expect all readers to agree with everything that is said — certainly there are parts that some professionals will find unpalatable and others may find parts indigestible. What, however, the book inescapably does, is to direct our attention to the subject and to start us questioning our motives, our procedures and our preparations for marketing.

Although it could be argued that marketing is the background against which the salesman makes his pitch, it is probably fair comment that the "perfect" marketer like the "perfect" salesman is born with some spark inside him rather than education being everything. The challenge this book addresses is to turn the spark into a successful blaze; it is only by analysis of the subject and careful consideration of the principles that success will be achieved.

It is for that reason that I commend Ted Cleaveley's writings as suitable material for the enquiring mind that expects to pursue its education; it calls for further deliberations and study to apply the principles to practice.

London, June 1984   Paul Orchard-Lisle

Contents Page No.

CHAPTER 1 INTRODUCTION 1
  1.1 The Property Institutions 4
  1.2 Objectives 7
  1.3 Marketing for the surveyor 9
  1.4 The RICS examination syllabus 11

CHAPTER 2 MARKETING 13
  2.1 Selling 15
  2.2 Marketing Planning 18
  2.3 Strategic Marketing Planning in the professional practice 21

CHAPTER 3 THE MARKET 27
  3.1 The current market 27
  3.2 The consumers of property 31
  3.3 Demand 33
  3.4 Estimating current demand 36
  3.5 Estimating future demand 37
  3.6 Implications for the surveyor 39
  3.7 The future market 40

CHAPTER 4 THE PRODUCT 43
  4.1 The buyers 43
  4.2 The property lifecycle 48
  4.3 Presentation of premises 51
  4.4 Product pricing 56
  4.5 New Product Development 58

CHAPTER 5 MARKETING THE PRACTICE 61
  5.1 Image 64
  5.2 The competitive edge 65
  5.3 Image building 72
  5.4 Attacking the market 75

		Page No.
CHAPTER 6	**MARKET RESEARCH**	79
6.1	Property development	81
6.2	The role of market research	86
6.3	Market research procedure	87
6.4	Implications for the property profession	89
6.5	The use of a research agency	91
6.6	An example	92
CHAPTER 7	**MARKET SEGMENTATION AND TARGETING**	95
7.1	Market segmentation	96
7.2	Targeting	100
7.3	Implications for the surveyor	100
CHAPTER 8	**PROMOTION**	103
8.1	Advertising	109
8.2	Public Relations	115
8.3	Sales promotion	119
8.4	Budgeting	127
8.5	Monitoring and control	128
CHAPTER 9	**SELLING**	133
9.1	What is selling?	135
9.2	Implications for the commercial practice	137
9.3	The salesman	140
9.4	Sales management	145
9.5	The sales office	148
CHAPTER 10	**SUMMARY AND CONCLUSIONS**	153
10.1	Summary	153
10.2	Recent marketing developments	158
10.3	The future	161
INDEX		165

List of Figures

	Page No.
Figure 1. Channels of persuasion.	*16*
Figure 2. Strategic Market Planning — the calculator market and Texas Instruments.	*19*
Figure 3. Boston Consulting Group — Business Portfolio Matrix.	*20*
Figure 4. The strategic management and marketing process.	*22*
Figure 5. Supply/Demand curve.	*35*
Figure 6. Product lifecycle. Normal pattern.	*50*
Figure 7. Product lifecycle. "Cycle-recycle" pattern.	*50*
Figure 8. Product lifecycle. Property pattern.	*50*
Figure 9. The property "product" lifecycle.	*52*
Figure 10. Factors influencing the location decision.	*54*
Figure 11. The role of market research in development appraisal.	*94*
Figure 12. Effectiveness of promotional methods.	*105*
Figure 13. Effectiveness of promotional methods at buyer readiness stages.	*106*
Figure 14. Promotional plan for a new development scheme.	*108*
Figure 15. Sales force performance under different remuneration packages.	*146*

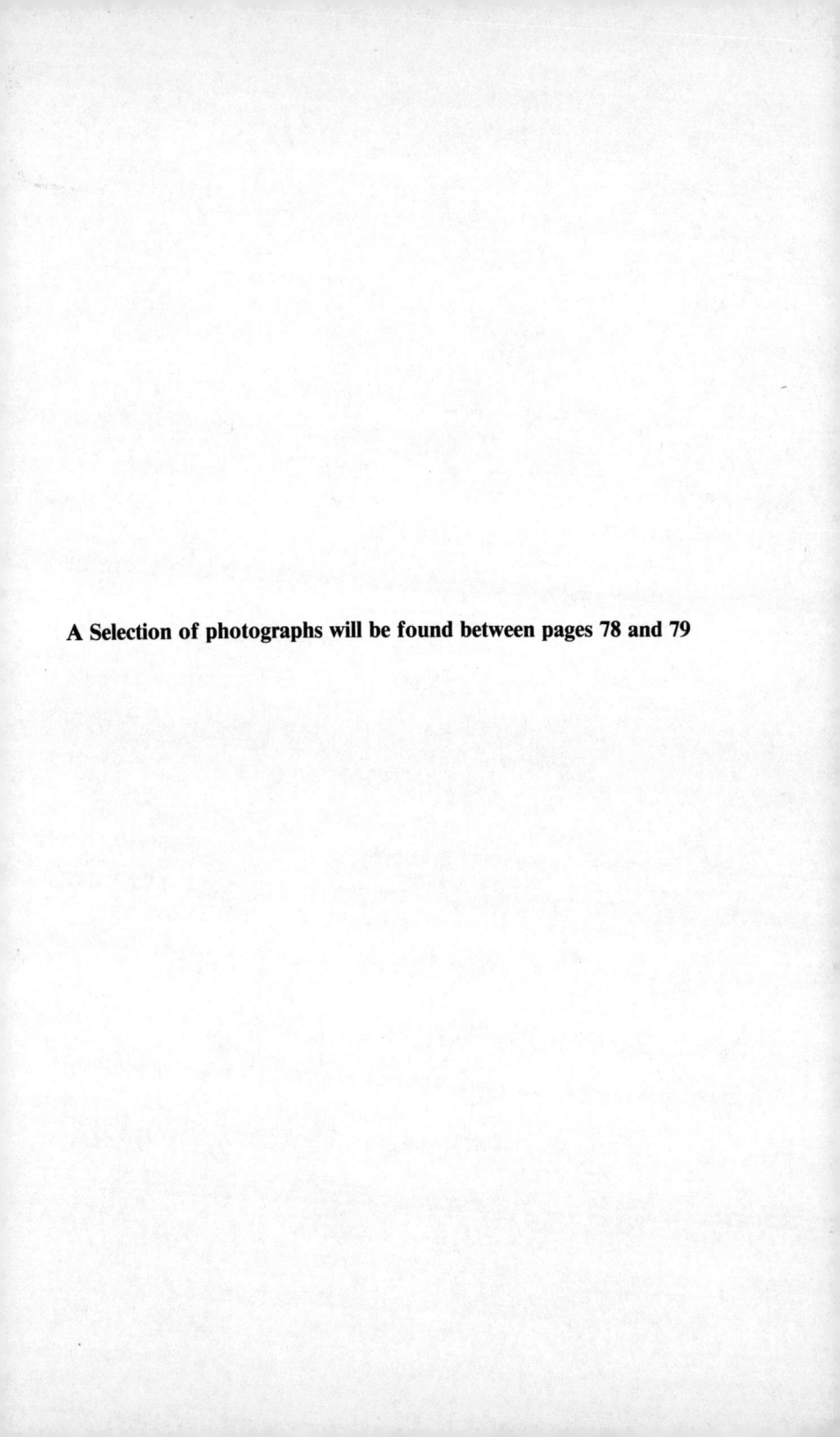

A Selection of photographs will be found between pages 78 and 79

CHAPTER 1
Introduction

Marketing as a professional business activity has only recently started to make an impact upon the commercial and industrial activities of Great Britain. Even now things are not as good as they could be — so many large and small companies in this country follow a commercial policy inevitably doomed to failure as a result of the inability to recognise the importance of marketing in their business. Based upon the simple premise that all civilised individuals need and want to own material products of all kinds, from wine to houses, in order to portray an image of success, comfort and well-being, marketing incorporates every aspect of consumerism in a capitalist society. Only in suppressed societies is this human need not allowed due fulfilment. Marketing is a "free-world" philosophy, totally misunderstood in suppressed societies: it is based to a large extent upon an appreciation of human emotion and depends upon being able to satisfy a desire in order to earn its place in the modern business environment.

How then have so many industries and professions been so successful for the last 100 years or more if marketing is such a recent discipline? Historically, the marketplace for all consumer and industrial goods on a worldwide scale has never been as depressed as it is now. Most market analysts accept that a cyclical pattern does exist where a recession of some severity occurs on a global basis every 15 years or so. The impression today is that world trading conditions will never return to "normal". Certainly, in the United Kingdom the prospects for re-opening major steel-works or shipyards are extremely bleak and, in fact, many plants have been demolished.

A hundred years ago, consumer demand for goods was buoyant. Great Britain had the skills, finance and low overheads, especially in manpower and energy, to provide the rest of the world with low-cost quality products. As long as demand exceeded supply, British manufacturers could sell products easily. Industrial and commercial property was in demand, planning restrictions were non-existent and with this boom came the emergence of the property surveyor, valuer and auctioneer. Professional services of all kinds grew in prominence, giving rise to the finest professional societies in the world, soon to obtain enviable status with royal charters and to act as a model for all foreign and colonial copies.

Over the last 30 years, however, things have changed and British industry has found itself facing increased labour costs, effective foreign competition and a variable level of consumer demand both at home and abroad. The death-blow for many has come during the last decade with a four-fold increase in the price of oil and the phenomenal rise of Japan, Taiwan and Korea as producers of cheap good-quality consumer and industrial products on a massive scale.

As a business activity, marketing has been around throughout this turbulent time, and it is only now that it has rightly risen to ascendancy. Increased competition, a more sophisticated consumer and the demand for technological advancement have combined to bring the marketing professional to a senior position in commerce and industry. There are very few successful companies without a marketing professional at a top management level with considerable responsibility for influencing the companies' profitable growth and development.

It is ironic that this country's main competitors overseas should have initially acquired their manufacturing and business skills from us, only now to exploit and develop them to our economic detriment. The president of the Confederation of British Industry, Sir Campbell Frazer, during his opening remarks at the 1982 annual conference at Eastbourne asked why British industry still "failed to get the marketing right" and how we allowed foreign companies to take our ideas and exploit them. To ask such a question of representatives of the greatest commercial tradition in the world seems incredible. Yet the truth is that many British companies are still concerned with the "product" rather than the "customer".

This syndrome, virtually unknown in Japan, is called "product orientation". In simple terms, the preoccupation with the excellence of a product in terms of technological design or quality replaces the recognition of a market that will actually buy it. An example of such a "technology push" is the development and production of a soft plastic drinks container by Imperial Chemical Industries (Plastics Division) in the late 1960s. Despite the competition from glass and metal containers and the evidence from market research that showed some consumer resistance, the product was seen as a technological breakthrough and subsequently developed by the plastics experts at ICI. After failing to secure one major customer in two years and with development expenditure exceeding £3m, the ICI main board killed the project.

Introduction

By comparison, a Japanese company would not have attempted to make the product without clearly establishing a consumer demand and then calculating that the demand could be satisfied at a profit. This approach is known as "market orientation".

Another aspect which has influence upon the property professions concerns not products but services. Traditionally, professional practices such as those of solicitors, accountants and engineers, as well as surveyors and valuers, have succeeded by operating in an environment where their specialised skills are in demand. During times of economic boom, such professional practices had a monopoly over the use of their particular skills and were generally regarded by the mass of the public as being both intellectually superior and essential as advisers or consultants. These professions gradually evolved their own language and mystique designed to carve out and ensure a niche in the commercial life of the country. Scales of fees and charges for services were devised and agreed by groups of individuals who, by joining together as institutions, achieved a level of protectionism still with us today. Little attention was ever paid to consumer demand and "buyers" rarely questioned the apparent necessity of using professional services.

A whole battery of government and consumer investigations have been instigated over the years, and many observers believe that with the improvement in educational standards, the rise of the "technocrat" and the influence of the mass media, many professional services are going to find things difficult during the next decade. The 1970s saw the emergence of "cut-price" estate agents, dismissed by many surveyors as being only a temporary unwelcome intrusion into the industry and yet serious enough to be mentioned by the Monopolies Commission in their investigation into the profession in 1969. There seems little doubt that the level of charges for professional services and the way in which those services are provided leaves a great deal to be desired as far as public image is concerned.

Marketing has a strong role to play here. The presentation of services in a convincing and clear way as well as showing a measure of enthusiasm and interest both in vendor and purchaser can make the difference between a successful and a mediocre professional. Services can be marketed in an environment which is already starting to question the value of the retained commercial agent. Recent experience in the industrial property market has seen direct marketing by developers (following perhaps a Barratt Homes approach) and the appointment of full-time sales staff working directly for the development company.

In this initial phase of Chapter 1 I have tried briefly to set the scene for a book on property marketing by first discussing the evolvement of marketing in the history of British industry and by pointing out the essential differences between "product orientation" and "market orientation". The need to market professional services more effectively is clearly illustrated by very recent developments, and in subsequent chapters I shall explain how lessons can be learned from the residential market and adapted to industrial and commercial property. This I will call "customer orientation" as all persons who buy a service or pay a fee are customers.

1.1 The Property Institutions

Among the traditional professional property institutions, marketing has been viewed with suspicion and a belief that the philosophy is inapplicable to the particular vocation of that institute. It has never been clearly understood that marketing is about identifying and satisfying consumer needs, and it tends to be confused with advertising, promotion or selling. Within the Royal Institution of Chartered Surveyors and the Incorporated Society of Valuers and Auctioneers marketing is only just beginning to make an impact. This is due to a number of historical and traditional reasons, some of which have been touched upon and others that will become apparent during subsequent chapters.

Despite differences in the background and training of surveyors or valuers and marketers, the truth is that many professional practices have been successfully marketing both their services and their clients' property for a long time. This will have been achieved by instinct rather than by training, as until recently training in the selling of professional services and the letting of property was covered only briefly under other subject areas.

Europe's largest house agents, Mann & Co, have decided to adopt an aggressive, imaginative policy in selling themselves. For example, by experimenting with local radio as an advertising media in the Reading area. This move follows a critical analysis of the results of local newspaper advertising and a genuine concern for their public image as a professional company.

Many small agents fear the recent moves by Lloyds Bank in purchasing good-quality estate agents to create the "Black Horse Agencies" group. Mann & Co seem to view this development as a means by which Lloyds can further promote their financial services. I would not be so complacent. Like most high-street banks, Lloyds have had surplus profits to spend and, apart from seeming to be determined to take away the current 60% share of the mortgage market held by building societies, have an experienced, well-financed marketing machine that will be looking for situations to exploit in the residential property field. For the first time in its history, the "marketing" function of the chartered surveyor is under seige by an experienced non-property-trained professional. Banks may be only the first of many commercial organisations to feel that they have both the skill and expertise to market property of all kinds, not just residential.

In his book *The Practice of Estate Agency*[1] published in 1980, Nigel Stephens, himself a Fellow of the RICS, makes several important points in his introduction. He warns against the dangers of shortsightedness and indicates concern for the lack of marketing skills of the professional practices in today's property market. He stresses that "agents have no monopoly on property and cannot afford to be complacent". While Nigel Stephens' book concerned itself only with the housing market, many of the points made above are equally applicable to commercial and industrial property. Such is the concern of the RICS and the College of Estate Management about the lack of training in marketing that the syllabus for the final examination in the General Practice Division now includes a section on marketing. A review of recent examination papers, however, shows no questions on the subject.

Nigel Stephens makes the point that an estate agency cannot be described as a "profession" in that it is not restricted by statute, although there are certain legal controls. No one professional body dominates "agency" work in total, and despite the vast majority of practices having a membership of either RICS or ISVA, neither of these bodies have devoted enough time to the training of members in the sale and letting of property. Yet even at this stage, the RICS syllabus is far from comprehensive and only broadly covers the subject. It certainly excludes any reference to the way in which marketing can be used to promote more effectively the image of the surveyor himself or the professional services of his practice.

There are obvious dangers in ignoring marketing and not placing sufficient emphasis on training students in this discipline. Nigel Stephens had this clearly at the back of his mind when he wrote that "entering [the house agency business] is easy and requires neither qualification or previous experience". While I find this a little hard to believe in that some property experience must be essential, the emergence of "cut-price" agents may be just one more step towards the growth of a completely new breed of "customer-orientated" property professionals.

Other professions are also under attack, for example the legal profession with the development of conveyancing companies. The recent submission to government by building societies suggests the commencement of not only a mortgage war with the high-street banks but also a deliberate attempt to offer a package deal to customers by having the ability to undertake other services such as conveyancing. In my view, it is only a matter of time before banks, building societies, or some similar kind of organisation are marketing a complete service to the consumer, from selling the property through to financing, conveyancing and maybe even to arranging furniture removal.

My investigations into commercial agency practice have revealed a disturbing trend which can only be described as a form of professional self-deception. Many property surveyors believe that they are both marketers and salesmen and scorn any attempts to point out that these claims cannot be justified by either their professional training or practice. The fact that property is successfully developed and let does not automatically make the surveyor or valuer involved a property marketing expert.

However, the profession does recognise that given the right location, any development will eventually let. There is perhaps nothing really clever about letting an office development in central London or a warehouse near a motorway junction, and few would claim that giving typed details of houses in popular areas to customers who walk into the agent's office has anything to do with the property profession at all.

The old saying "location, location and location" still holds true to an extent for many purchasers, but the trend is changing. It is this change that finds the surveyor and valuer so ill-prepared, because only the application of modern marketing techniques will enable changes to be recognised and exploited.

The change is being brought about by such things as:
— increases in operating costs
— new technology demanding different facilities
— the concern of new industries about image
— new communications technology
— demands of the workforce for lifestyle and environment.

The whole market is dynamic, not static, but again I find many property professionals convinced that they know all about markets and need no special training or advice. While I accept that being active in the market place as a salesman is a major input to market analysis, this is no substitute for market research, which all successful enterprises in the western world recognise as an essential ingredient to commercial success. In the property profession, many believe that market research is to do with soap powder and has no role in property developments and letting, especially in the commercial and industrial field.

This quaint and potentially dangerous view also appears to be supported by some developers and architects who choose to seek the professional advice of agents on such matters as market demand. Despite the fact that many commercial agents are generally incapable of undertaking any real market analysis, by virtue of lack of training, experience and attitude, the architect may still believe this to be a better bet than commissioning, say, a market research firm to do the work.

How many commercial agents can say to the architect or developer, "No, there is no market for your proposal and here is the evidence for this statement". We all know that all sites with planning permission will be developed at some stage but that the decision may not be based on market forces. If the site is in a prime location and lets quickly then the agent may claim to be a "marketing" expert. If the development is in the wrong location and is therefore slow to let, the agent will maintain that "the market is quiet" or that "demand has slackened off". A reduction in asking rent may show a flurry of lettings which the agent will claim is due to his marketing expertise rather than the fact that the units were overpriced in the first place. A real marketer would have established the right rental by research before the development was even designed.

At the end of the day it is not the agent's money that is at risk, it is the developer's, and with all advertising and brochure costs also being paid by the client, one wonders exactly what does motivate an agent.

Residential practice has been totally excluded from this discussion as I consider that a disturbing number of agents in this field are thoroughly deserving of the criticism leveled at them. Most residential agents are like mail-order houses but with half the efficiency. Yet even here at least some have finally recognised that the adoption of a marketing policy across the whole sphere of their activities will produce results thus giving their business a new start, with customer satisfaction as the main objective.

There may still be time to retrieve the situation and restore the general practice surveyor and valuer to his rightful position in the industrial and commercial property world. The modern "market-orientated" surveyor has no misunderstanding of his role, does not accept that there is any "professional versus commercial" conflict in the services he provides and firmly believes that his sole objective is to satisfy clients and customers by the provision of these services at a profit.

1.2 Objectives
In setting down the following objectives, I am conscious of the fact that many agency practices are successfully surviving the current

economically depressed times. Many surveyors and valuers are "natural" marketers, with considerable experience in the disposal of property, and will continue to adapt to market forces successfully. Nevertheless, it cannot be disputed that there is much room for improvement and while the training of the surveyor quite rightly involves a great deal of emphasis on other essential topics, the importance of marketing cannot be overlooked in today's business environment.

As a marketer, rather than a surveyor or valuer, I have had the unique opportunity of objectively and critically observing the marketing activities of the agent, especially in the commercial and industrial field. I have not, as yet, found one professional practice that has adopted a total marketing philosophy in its business, either in the offering of its professional services or in its approach to the disposal of property.

I sincerely hope that both students and practising professionals will glean some helpful tips from this book, which is intended to be a marketing handbook for the general practice surveyor and valuer. It should not be followed slavishly as marketers must be innovative and generate their own ideas. I remain firmly convinced that there is enormous potential in the proper application of marketing techniques to the property world.

The objectives of this piece of work can be described thus:

(a) To illustrate in simple terms the role that marketing has to play in the successful development of those practices who wish to grow and survive profitably.

(b) To act as a textbook for RICS and ISVA students who will be faced with having to earn a living in their chosen vocation.

(c) To dispel a number of myths about marketing, selling, advertising, promotion, etc, that are beginning to creep into property world conversation.

(d) To reassure those traditionalists who, understandably, feel threatened by the introduction of marketing into their practice or work ethic.

(e) To act as a spur to those who feel that there may be some value in the enthusiastic adoption of marketing techniques into their profession.

My intention is to give an all-round, simple description of modern marketing with emphasis throughout on how the property expert can use the techniques to his or her own advantage. The range of subsequent chapters extends from market research — always the first activity in the development of business — through to the last stages of selling the product.

1.3 Marketing for the surveyor

What does the marketing surveyor or valuer do to expand his knowledge beyond the scope of this book? There is value in considering membership of marketing or allied professional societies, in that meaningful contact would be made with marketers from other businesses. In addition, most societies organise various training courses on marketing and selling activities which most certainly have an application to the property profession. I have detailed below those that I have found to be of most value.

The Institute of Marketing

Membership of the Institute of Marketing is open to all persons involved in the marketing of consumer and industrial products or services. Full membership is obtained by examination and many polytechnics now run courses for the Diploma of Marketing which will qualify students for entry. There is also a scheme of entry for mature persons.

While not yet carrying a royal charter, the Institute of Marketing is the largest organisation of its kind in the United Kingdom and publishes an informative weekly magazine, appropriately called *Marketing*, which contains information and news on consumer and industrial products as well as features on particular companies or specialised services.

But it is the wide range of membership and its strong regional base that makes the institute so valuable in that new techniques successfully used in one market or business activity can rub off onto another, often with worthwhile results.

Another activity of the Institute of Marketing is its organisation of seminars and training courses. Subjects range from "How to make sales presentations" to "Direct mail" and "Strategic market planning" and vary from one-day sessions to seven-day residential courses at the institute's own college near Maidenhead. The only slight reservation that a surveyor may feel is that the membership tends to be made up of persons from consumer industries, advertising agents, consultants and so on, despite an increasing representation from industrial companies. In no way should this be an inhibiting factor, as much can be learned from experienced marketing practitioners irrespective of their company or product. It should be remembered that the property profession is, after all, a relative newcomer to the marketing scene and has everything to gain by examining and exploiting the techniques available.

The Market Research Society (MRS)

The importance of market research has never been fully understood or acknowledged by the property profession. Yet this invaluable commercial activity is currently responsible for the design of our cars, the mix of our television programmes and the variety of our frozen food. Market research is the cornerstone of marketing and will be covered in detail in a subsequent chapter.

Members of the Market Research Society are practitioners in the art of understanding the consumer. They come from a range of activities including government, universities, social institutions, consumer and industrial companies, advertising agents and, of course, market research agencies. The width of experience in the examination of the consumer is remarkable and with its sister organisation the European Society of Marketing and Research, the MRS is now operating on an international scale with the membership capability to undertake market research in Japan, the Middle East or Africa.

Membership is obtained by examination or by an application supported by referees, and the member receives a monthly magazine with the opportunity to meet fellow researchers at London and regional meetings. Like the Institute of Marketing, the MRS organises seminars and presentations to further the skills of its members in this important field.

The property professional who wishes to use market research, especially in the residential sector, and to extend his skills in this activity, should seriously consider joining the society.

The Industrial Marketing Research Association (IMRA)

A sister organisation to the MRS, having close links and a membership which contains a proportion who are in both societies, the Industrial Marketing Research Association, as its name implies, tends to cater more for persons involved in industrial, rather than consumer, markets. Often operating in areas where little data is available and where the market is fragmented, IMRA members spend a lot of time undertaking what is termed "desk research", ie the examination of sales data, accounts, import/export statistics etc, as part of a research project. Their work also involves a great deal of interviewing of senior management.

This industrial bias has given rise to the development of special techniques which make IMRA membership rather more suited to the commercial property world. If asked to choose, I would recommend the MRS for residential agency surveyors or valuers and IMRA for the commercial and industrial side. Membership of IMRA is again by sponsored application.

Introduction 11

These three organisations give the marketing surveyor the opportunity to expand his knowledge and understanding of the subject and to mix with experienced professionals. The obtaining of membership need not involve a great deal of effort, and will repay an unbiased and enthusiastic involvement.

1.4 The RICS examination syllabus

At this point it is worthwhile putting into its context the relevant extract from the RICS General Practice examination syllabus on marketing. The entry is listed as number 5 in the syllabus and, appropriately enough, shares the slot with "management". Both are prefixed by the words "Estate Agency" clearly indicating where the examination board best considers the subject to be placed.

For reference purposes, I have broken the marketing syllabus down into sections against which are indicated the relevant chapters of this book. I hope that this will act as a quick guide to the reader.

"Characteristics of the United Kingdom property market" — see Chapter 3.

"The nature of marketing problems" — see Chapter 2.

"The monitoring and control of the agency office" — see Chapters 5 and 9.

"Multiple and sole agencies" — see Chapter 5.

"The marketing plan: mix; implementation of plan" — see Chapters 2 and 8.

"Sales forecast" — see Chapter 3.

"Pricing decision" — see Chapter 4.

"Approach to selling" — see Chapters 5 and 9.

"Consideration of sales particulars and auction catalogues" — see Chapter 8.

"Promotional decisions: determination of budget size; media decisions and sales promotion" — see Chapter 8.

"Technological advances and market changes" — see Chapters 3 and 7.

"The application of marketing principles to residential, commercial, industrial and special and overseas properties" — see whole book, but for principles see Chapters 1 and 3.

"Overseas marketing techniques" — see Chapter 2.

In formulating the syllabus, the examination board is expecting a broad, rather than detailed, understanding of the subject of marketing with particular emphasis on the agency role in the profession. It is generally felt that this view is too restrictive and may inhibit the surveyor who feels, quite rightly, that marketing has much wider implications for the whole property profession.

I sincerely hope that while covering all the aspects of the syllabus in detail, this work will give a wider insight into other marketing techniques that can be adopted successfully by both the student and the experienced professional.

References. Chapter 1.
[1] "The Practice of Estate Agency". Nigel Stephens. Estates Gazette. 1980.

CHAPTER 2
Marketing

The purpose of this chapter is to describe marketing in a simple way that will, hopefully, be understood by professionals who until recently have not been involved in the subject. In so doing, it is necessary to delve a little into the more technical aspects in order to provide the background needed for a clearer appreciation of how and why marketing is where it is today.

It is significant that Nigel Stephens should draw upon the views and definitions of two American professors in the text of his book dealing with marketing. This is perhaps not only a reflection of the RICS and ISVA past appreciation of the subject in thinking that marketing is only practised seriously across the Atlantic, but also a sad indication of how poorly the British marketing organisations have promoted themselves to the other professional institutions in this country.

Many excellent "home-grown" authors have written a succession of comprehensive books and reports on the subject of marketing. The Institute of Marketing itself has been around since the sixties and publishes a large amount of very readable material. As a full member of the institute, I am embarrassed by the fact that Nigel Stephens makes no mention of the Institute of Marketing.

For my part I shall draw upon British sources of information: reference to the American approach to property marketing will come later.

The established definition of marketing, used by the Institute of Marketing, is as follows: "Marketing is the management process responsible for identifying, anticipating and satisfying customer requirements profitably". An immediate reaction from the property professionals might be that this definition does not apply to their industry, since the agent is not selling a product as such but is acting as the person who advises property owners and brings about a transfer of the ownership of property. You will note, however, that the definition does not mention the word "product" but does specify "requirements". A customer's requirements may be for a service *or* for a product, or both. In either case, the accepted definition of marketing applies. An agency should have the ability to satisfy customer requirements profitably both in terms of the provision of professional services and in the successful disposal of clients' property.

The definition also uses the word "identifying" in terms of customer requirements. This means that the needs and expectations of the "end-user" must be established *before* a product or service is provided. While it is often possible to stimulate demand for new products such as the introduction of video cassette recorders, generally most profitable new markets are developed from the recognition of a "need" which is not being satisfied. This may be termed the "market gap". For example, there was clearly a market gap in the need for a cheap form of transport to encourage economic and social development of communities and countries, and Henry Ford identified that gap and designed a product that could be produced cheaply but would satisfy customer need at a profit.

In property terms, there are no sound reasons why customer needs should not be identified. I would suggest that the provision of property has always been based on every other criteria except a real understanding of consumer requirements. This is not entirely the fault of the property profession in that the designation of land for industrial, commercial and residential development is undertaken in this country by local authority planners not by surveyors. These arbitrary decisions are not based on consumer requirements, as a planner cannot be expected to understand the needs and expectations of end-users when a parcel of land is designated for a particular development. Given this restriction, however, sufficient land is available for the property man to get it right, whether he advises on the development, builds it, or sells the finished product. Why then is it that so much empty property is currently on the market? Is it due to world recession or the policy of the government in office? Is it what the market actually wants?

"Anticipating" customer requirements is another part of the definition. This has to do with forward planning and the provision of products or services at the right time and at the right price.

The Japanese motorcycle firm Honda got it right by identifying a need for a cheap, economical machine that could be customised to suit individuals. The product had to be a "fun" item as well as a means of transport. They also anticipated when this product would be "needed" in the USA and then in Europe, by taking into account the social and economic factors of each potential market sector. The world now knows how successful this strategy has been for Honda.

Much is being made in this country at present of high-technology industry and requirements for science parks. Have we correctly identified market requirements? When do we anticipate that new technology industries will want and be able to afford specialised buildings? It seems that no real market evidence is available and that it has been left to architects and developers in both the public and private sectors to attempt to satisfy these perceived markets by the provision of basic traditional premises differing only in headroom, finishes and landscaping.

The design and provision of shops and offices also still tends to follow traditional ideas based upon broad assumptions. For example, it is assumed that all companies wish to have offices in city centres, that rural locations are not viable, that the lock-up shop is still the best facility and so on. In his article on "Retail location through the 1980s", published in *Estates Gazette*[1], John Ratcliffe put the case quite precisely in referring to retail development trends: "Increasingly, the watchwords of successful retail development are selectivity, research and professionalism". He expands this by describing each element in his statement. "Selectivity" in terms of location and site suitability — certainly a traditional approach by any surveyor. "Research" with regard to market penetration and optimum trading mix: by this he seems to be stressing the value of market research in helping to ensure that the development blend will appeal to the market. Finally, "professionalism" in respect of effective project management and a marketing strategy. Again, project management should be the domain of the surveyor and yet the design and implementation of a marketing strategy for the successul disposal of the finished "product" is the very area in which the property surveyor finds himself unfortunately at a disadvantage.

2.1. Selling

If the above describes marketing, then what is selling? Why is the term "selling" so often mixed with marketing? How can so many large companies have a managerial position described as sales *and* marketing?

Selling can best be viewed as a tactical weapon in the marketing armoury. Other tactical weapons such as advertising join with selling to enable the marketer to achieve his objective of satisfying consumer requirements profitably in a particular market.

The sales organisation, irrespective of its size, is responsible for making the product or service available to the optimum number of consumers in that market. Selling is a component of promotion and is aptly described by Norman Hart in his book *Industrial Advertising and Publicity*[2] as a "channel of persuasion" in that it constitutes an effective means of communicating with and influencing a desired group of consumers. Figure 1 shows the relationship of selling with other channels of persuasion in the property marketing context.

In assessing the impact of a sales force when compared with other channels of persuasion, research by Hugh Buckner in 1967 as part of his book *How British Industry Buys*[3] showed that 66% of senior management up to board level considered that salesmen's visits were among the most important methods of obtaining information on products or services. By comparison, 14% rated advertising and 12% mailshots as effective methods — the two used mostly by property agents. The finance director of a company may consider that the maintenance of a sales force is an expense that cannot be afforded and yet research would seem to suggest that a sales force may be more cost-effective against advertising costs.

Fig. 1 Channels of persuasion

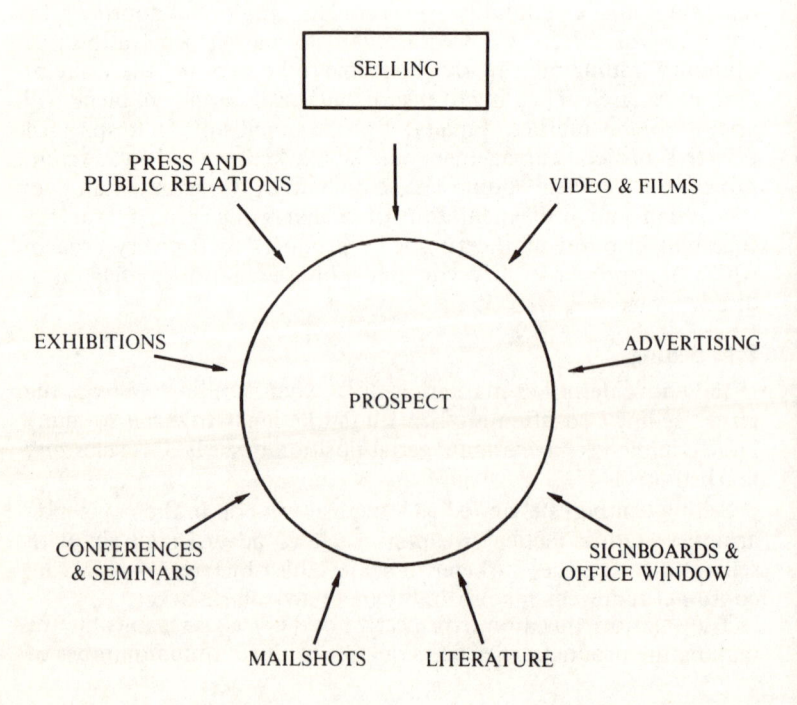

How does this relate to the surveyor or valuer? First the difference between marketing and selling should now be clear. Second, it must also be understood that marketing should be the overall function of any professional practice that wishes to grow profitably and that a sales force, an advertising campaign and mailshots are all methods of communication and persuasion. While advertising and mailshots are traditional activities of the professional practice, is it possible for the practice to operate an effective sales team? Would such a move generate extra business? The answers must be yes and yes. It is perfectly feasible for a surveyor or valuer to become a "salesman" as well; in fact it could be argued that sales activities are already part of property surveyors' functions. Yet surveyors and valuers are not *trained* in the art of selling.

The traditional view of a salesman in this country is based largely upon consumers' experience of the door-to-door and used-car kind, both of which do exist, often successfully. Other salesman images are associated with carpet warehouses and furniture stores where the impression is often gained that as a potential customer you are "selling" and the assistant is "buying" rather than the other way round. We have all had experience of the rude waiter, the scruffy ticket collector and the condescending receptionist. These are not salesmen; they are nothing more than information providers or "order-takers".

This poor image of the salesman unfortunately seems to have led the professional institutions of this country to adopt a very unreal understanding of the role of their members, resulting in an indifferent attitude to the consumer. I suspect that few accountants, civil engineers or surveyors would consider themselves to be salesmen as well as professional experts, and yet they fully expect to make a decent living by charging customers a fee for a service provided. Many agents refer to property being "marketed" rather than sold — a further misuse of terminology.

More and more we see the basic art of selling being shrouded in clever terminology. Sales consultants, technical representatives and field operators are frequently in evidence in today's commercial activities and, while I accept that jobs do vary marginally, all these persons are involved in one basic task — selling. No individual with the minimum of understanding of commerce and industry should ever underrate the salesman — the person upon whom this country depends for its very existence, as long as we are a trading nation. In the context of this book, selling has a vital role to play in the successful development of a surveyor's career and of his practice.

Without the salesman the marketing function is crippled and unable to achieve its objectives.

2.2. Marketing Planning

In order to implement an effective marketing policy it is necessary to undertake an amount of forward planning. All businesses must plan ahead in an attempt to foresee cash-flow problems, anticipate when a market is ready to break into and when to invest in new plant or products. To be successful, I believe that professional practices also need to plan ahead and to do this it is necessary to understand the broad principles of market planning and its strategic implications.

The word strategic in the sense of market planning relates to the overall objectives of the company or partnership and how these are to be successfully achieved. Markets are dynamic and need constant monitoring. Thus effective strategic market planning has one great and invincible feature: flexibility. Within the overall objectives of a business, often referred to as the corporate or company plan, several options should be built in to allow for both optimistic and pessimistic circumstances that may occur. Although very desirable, it is extremely difficult to allow enough flexibility in strategic market planning to allow for the unexpected. An example of this in recent times would be the forecast of the sale of dishwashers in Europe. The forecast was broadly based on the expected cost of raw materials and the amount of personal disposable income of the householder. Between 1973 and 1978 the price of oil increased four times, adversely affecting both raw materials and income. The result has been a disaster for the dishwasher manufacturer.

Strategic market planning is today an integral part of management practice and is being successfully adopted by many companies. Texas Instruments have achieved spectacular results in the calculator market in this country by good market planning. Texas researched the potential market and divided it into "segments" based upon consumer characteristics and their requirements. They then systematically attacked each segment with the right kind of calculator at the right price, allowing for and anticipating the timing of changes in demand. For example, Texas decided that there was little profit in making a calculator for older schoolchildren until the authorities permitted the devices to be used during school lessons or examinations. Once this was agreed in 1981 Texas school calculators were in the shops. The graph in Figure 2 shows Texas Instruments growth in sales in this lucrative market.

Marketing planning is preceded by a consideration of the company's long-term objectives and strategies for survival. This is referred to by Philip Kotler in his book *Marketing Management* —

Analysis, Planning and Control[4] as "the strategic management process" and is fundamental to the successful contribution and growth of any business or enterprise.

Where strategic management and market planning combine is in the achievement of company goals and objectives. In the professional practice, the strategic management process will comprise the detailed consideration of how the practice intends to grow, if that is the partners' intention, or, more appropriately, how it is to survive into the 1990s. The key task in the management process is the company's examination of itself as a commercial organisation in a way that clarifies thinking and allows for each component to be critically examined.

These components are described by Kotler as "strategic business units" and are assessed in terms of their share of the particular market and their contribution to profit of the company or group. For the surveyor or valuer, a strategic business unit could be a branch office or a particular professional service offered by the practice.

Fig. 2. Strategic Market Planning — the calculator market and Texas Instruments

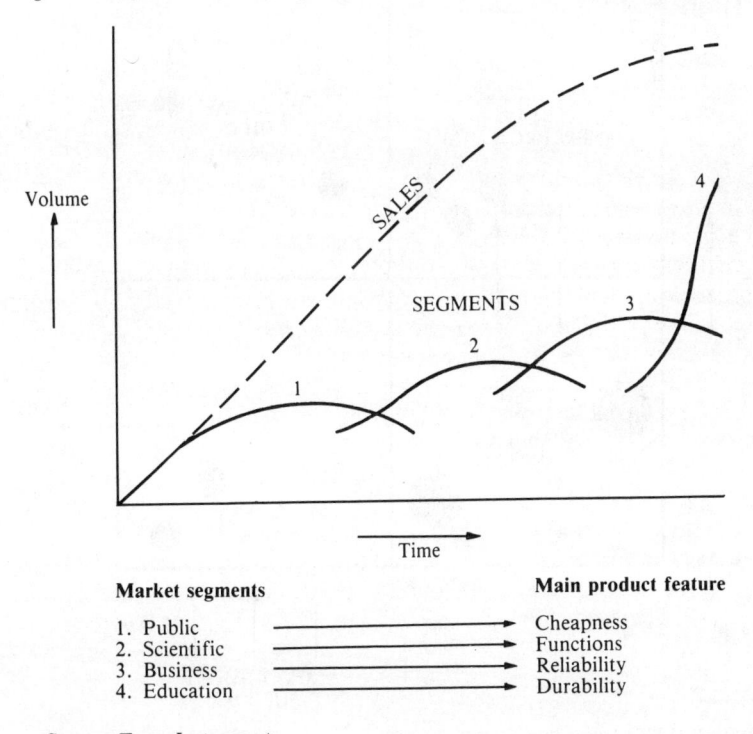

Market segments	Main product feature
1. Public	Cheapness
2. Scientific	Functions
3. Business	Reliability
4. Education	Durability

Source: Texas Instruments

20 *The Marketing of Industrial and Commercial Property*

An approach to this critical assessment developed by the Boston Consulting Group uses what is termed a Business Portfolio Matrix. This is shown in Figure 3. It can be seen that each strategic business unit is located in the matrix according to its relative market share and the growth of that market. The area of each circle is proportional to annual sales, or fees. A market share of 0.4 in this example shows that the business unit has 40% of the market and yet its size may indicate little revenue-earning capacity. It may in fact be "going to the dogs", hence the term used.

Fig. 3. Boston Consulting Group — Business Portfolio Matrix

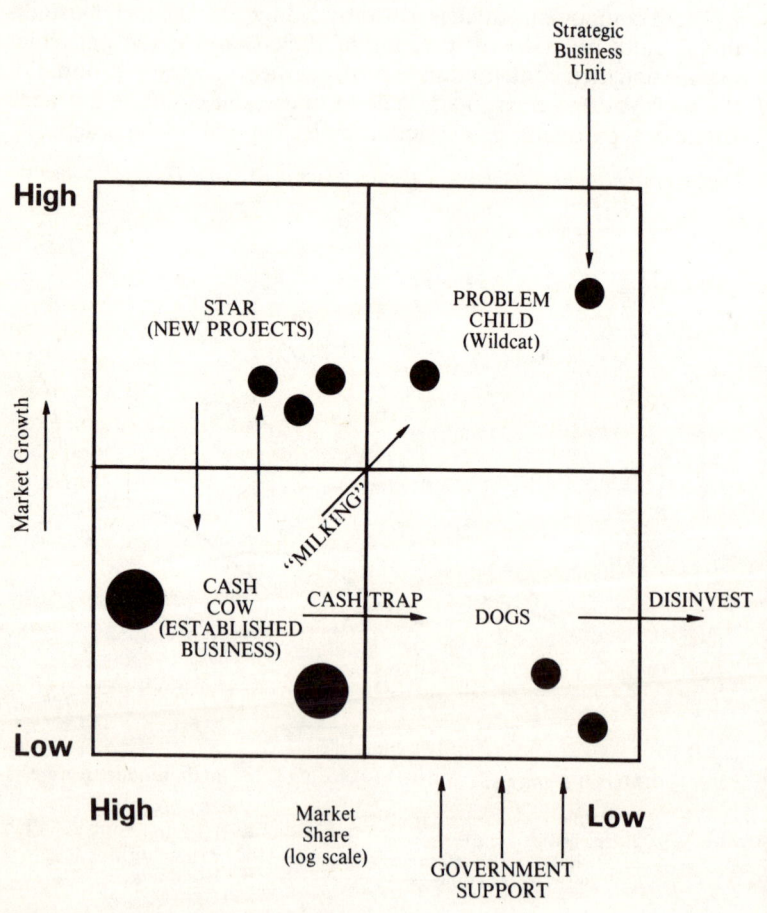

Source: Boston Consulting Group

"Stars" are in high-growth-rate markets and may eventually become "cash-cows", which are the main income business units of the company. "Problem children" require serious consideration by management as they often require heavy financial support to maintain market shares. The distribution of strategic business units in the matrix shows the company's state of health at that time.

The General Electric Company goes further by developing a nine-cell matrix that brings in other aspects important to success connected with the "attractiveness" of a particular market and the ability of a company to compete in that market.

A good example of the application of this concept in the property profession is the view taken by a residential practice of, say, the agricultural market. While the practice will possibly have chartered surveyors as partners, dealing in the agricultural market requires special skills and experience. The Black Horse Agency's approach would be to acquire partnerships with these skills rather than trying to develop the expertise within the group.

2.3. Strategic Marketing Planning in the professional practice

As with any industrial or consumer product company, the professional property practice can benefit by thinking and acting strategically. Certain aspects are inappropriate for the property industry, while others may apply differently, but what is without doubt is the overriding need for the professional surveyor or valuer to start thinking like a marketer rather than a professional expert *if* it is his or her intention to "satisfy consumer requirements at a profit".

The main business activities of a chartered surveyor's practice fall into three categories: professional advisory services including project and portfolio management; the disposal of all types of property; and, for most practices, advising retained clients on the acquisition of investments. For the purposes of strategic planning, all three can, I feel, be considered together in that each may not exist without the other, bearing in mind that a number of readers of this book may be running a successful property disposal business without wanting to offer expert consultancy or advice to clients.

In developing a business portfolio matrix, therefore, it may be that certain strategic business units deemed to be under the general property market "umbrella" are missing for some practices. How long they are missing will depend upon the purpose and objectives of the practice and the ability of the organisation to identify and exploit market opportunities.

The raw material of marketing planning is demand or sales forecasting, an area fraught with danger for the inexperienced. The implications for the property expert and for the future marketing of premises are such that I have devoted a large part of Chapter 3 to this subject. The input of forecasting takes place at the "analysis of market opportunity" stage because it constitutes a methodical attempt to predict sales and profits in a number of potential markets at a given future date.

A further aspect of extreme importance to the surveyor is to do with the "product" itself, that is, the property or groups of properties. Chapter 4 will cover this key factor in more detail. At this stage, we should concern ourselves with the value of strategic management and market planning to the practice itself and with the way in which the full range of consultancy and agency services can be developed.

In Figure 4 I have attempted to construct a flow diagram specifically for the professional practice. The steps taken in this combined planning process are as follows:

(1) Definition of objectives of the practice.
(2) Examination of business portfolio.
(3) Search for markets.
(4) Segmenting the market.
(5) Establish a competitive edge.
(6) Design the marketing and monitoring structure.
(7) Develop the marketing plan.
(8) Implement the plan
(9) Review achievement and evaluate results.

The figure shows these nine stages to have a number of external and internal factors providing input at each stage. It is essential to properly consider the implications of each input before moving to the next stage. A number of inputs can come from within the practice itself, where there should be a fund of knowledge on most aspects, others will require the commissioning of outside specialists. None of these steps or procedures are beyond the capability of a professional practice intending to develop its business profitably.

1. Definition of objectives

The partnership considers what it is in business for and what its goals are. It must take into account the effect of government policy, the state of the property market and the requirements and aspirations of the practice's "stakeholders".

The current business environment must also be examined by the partners so that both optimistic and pessimistic extremes can be considered in terms of the implications for business development. For example, the entry of Lloyds Bank into estate agency could constitute an environmental "shock" for the property agency profession: civil war in Saudi Arabia would be the same for European industry and would, in turn, affect the disposal of property.

2. Examination of business portfolio

A critical and objective assessment of the components of the practice and their revenue earning capacity is the next step. It is important to estimate market shares and growths, together with a broad attempt to identify opportunities for expansion. This will provide the marketing team with a framework within which a detailed analysis of market potential can be undertaken. The partners must also take into account any financial constraints to development and specify these to the marketing team.

I believe that the outcome of this phase is the adoption of one of three strategies. A "do-nothing" strategy involves no changes, concentrating only on the desire to "stay alive". This negative approach to business planning is very common and if used perpetually, leads to loss of market share and eventual bankruptcy. The benefit of a "do-nothing" policy is that it does not require any action by the partners, who would instead tend to resort to the view that "things will turn out all right when the market picks up".

A retrenchment strategy seeks to dispose of business units that are no longer profitable or use up too much revenue from the "cash-cows" of the practice. This strategy results in redundancies and expenditure cut-backs which, unless they are really carefully considered on a long-term basis, take the form of "fire-fighting" rather than planning measures.

The third strategy is positive and constitutes a real attempt by the partners to diversify and exploit the practices and skills of their staff. A number of feasible business opportunities would be identified and passed to the marketing team for examination and report. This feedback can be requested on an agreed time-scale so that the marketers in the practice are regularly putting reports and ideas back to senior management. In the examination of new opportunities, the marketers will come up with innovations and side issues, all of which should be encouraged for discussion.

3. Search for markets

This is the first major activity of the marketing team and forms the detailed investigation of ideas put forward by the management team. This phase also evaluates the skills and resources available and commissions specialists to report on various markets. A look at potential demand for services or sales of properties would, in my opinion, be more meaningful as a joint venture between the practice's own experts and an independent consultant.

4. Segmenting the market

Effective segmentation allows the practice to target different markets more effectively and to utilise properly the variety of skills and resources available. The marketers will at this stage be able to determine if the markets with the greatest potential for the practice are actually capable of being segmented and targeted.

5. Establish a competitive edge

Next comes the determination of which aspects of the practice's service will make it more "attractive" to the consumer than those of a competitor. This may take a multitude of forms, which, when joined together, give a valid impression of the practice as being consumer-orientated and professional. Creative thinking and imaginative flair is required here. The services of a sales promotion specialist or advertising agency can often be useful at this point to put forward new ideas.

The competitive edge may vary, depending upon the particular segment of the market that has been targeted by the practice. For example, with the residential market, aspects such as office style, staff and personal attention may be considered. For the investment client, market research and presentation may be areas in which the practice feels it can steal a march on its competitors. Having determined which markets to attack and the practice's competitive position, it is essential to establish the overall pricing policy at this stage. The senior management will have already modified their thinking to take account of financial constraints in phase 2 but at this stage charges, costs and remunerations must be agreed before the design of a marketing system is considered.

6. Design the marketing systems

This phase involves setting up the actual detailed procedure by which the particular target market is to be approached. Marketing systems design is the task of establishing a marketing organisation, together with an information, planning and control system that will accomplish the objectives at minimum cost.

Much will depend on the availability of resources and skills — perhaps recruitment will be necessary — and there are obviously implications for management in ensuring that all the necessary support and administrative services are available.

7. Develop the marketing plan

The marketing plan is the written document that sets down the objectives of the practice in each target market, the tactics to be used and the results the practice is seeking. This operational manual is a record of the culmination of the thinking and the decisions of all concerned in its formulation.

Goals, or estimated levels of achievement are specified in the plan (in effect, sales targets) and a budget is allocated. The term "marketing mix", referred to in the RICS examination syllabus, appears at this phase. In the consumer industry, the marketing mix is often known as the "four Ps" — product, price, promotion and place.

8. Implement the plan

A marketing plan is nothing unless it can be properly implemented by the staff responsible for specific tasks within specific time periods. As Philip Kotler says: "Implementation requires good and continuous communication up and down the management ladder as well as across". It is also essential that management controls the implementation of the plan in terms of performance and profitability.

Flexibility is as important in plan implementation as it is throughout the strategic marketing process. The practice must react to changes in the target market and must be prepared for contingencies. Marketing strategies can date quickly, even in a non-volatile market such as property.

9. Review and evaluate

This phase completes the cycle of management and market planning by forcing those managers responsible to report back on the results of implementation. It also provides a means by which the marketing team can communicate to the partnership the need for a change in direction on any particular aspect of plan implementation.

In subsequent chapters I will detail certain stages of the planning process and attempt to relate the activities to agency practice in particular.

References. Chapter 2.

[1] "Retail location through the 1980s". John Ratcliffe. Estates Gazette 13th November 1982.

[2] "Industrial Advertising and Publicity". Norman Hart. Associated Business Programmes Ltd. 1978.

[3] "How British Industry Buys" Hugh Buckner. Hutchinson. 1967.

[4] "Marketing Management — Analysis, Planning and Control". Philip Kotler. Prentice/Hall International 1980.

CHAPTER 3
The Market

In order for us to pursue the study of the application of modern marketing techniques to the property profession, it is necessary to examine in brief detail the state of the property market as it stood in 1983. It is not my intention to quote vast tables of statistics — these are detailed in other publications already available — but rather to view the market in the way the senior partners of a practice should when preparing for a strategic management meeting.

The importance of informed opinion among very experienced professionals should never be under-estimated, and I have taken the opportunity to quote several opinion leaders in various property fields who have kindly given their permission for the purpose. I have concentrated on industrial and commercial property but have also nodded in the direction of residential in passing, as there are considerable areas of similarity in terms of marketing.

Reading a wealth of material in this way gives one a different view of the situation in that most professionals agree in broad terms about the depressed state of the market yet seem to be unable to offer a positive view on what should be done, resorting instead to a series of stated objectives all of which are totally respectable but not necessarily achievable. This may be due to the problems of an over supply of good-quality premises, the fact that the market is beyond the point of possible stimulation, or perhaps that most practitioners find themselves in a market which they are uncertain about or feel that they do not have the necessary skills and resources to cope with.

3.1. The current market

(a) Industrial

Between December 1979 and December 1982, vacant industrial floorspace increased from 53m to 107m sq ft, a rise of 100%. This estimate of vacancy by King & Co[1] indicates the depressed state of the market linked, according to Michael Bellegarde of King & Co, to United Kingdom unemployment levels. Bernard Thorpe & Partners' 1982 industrial floorspace survey[2] indicated that 34m sq ft of this vacant space was in the 32 London boroughs of which 8m sq ft was available on a freehold basis.

The trend towards the over-provision of new small units is indicated by Table 1, showing Thorpe's calculations of vacant units by size and age in the London boroughs. It is interesting to note that nearly 30% of vacant units in September 1982 were new unused premises. There is perhaps a parallel here with the supply and demand of residential property referred to later in this chapter. The figure of 47% of space in units of 20,000 sq ft or more may contain a high proportion of obsolete property.

Looking nationally again, the total stock of industrial/warehousing space in England in 1980 amounted to 345m sq ft, according to the Department of the Environment statistics published that year, an increase of about 10% since 1975. The accelerated increase in vacant stock indicated by King & Co would suggest a large slice of second-hand premises coming onto the market.

The average size of an industrial/warehouse unit in 1977 was 31,000 sq ft. Despite a number of surrenders of large outdated premises, this average size had not increased noticeably by 1980, and no less than 308,000 units of industrial or warehouse space formed the total stock at this time. Taking King & Co's figure of 107m sq ft vacant and the DOE's average size for each hereditament as constant between 1980 and 1982, one can calculate a very rough total of 3,400 industrial/warehouse units available for disposal at the beginning of 1983.

Table 1. Vacant industrial floorspace in the London boroughs, September 1982.

Size band (sq ft)	% of new units	% of total available
Under 5,000	51	13
5,000-12,500	36	24
12,500-20,000	7	17
20,000 or more	6	47

Age of property	% of total available
New	30
1970-1980	39
1950-1969	10
1940-1949	15
Pre-1910	6

Source: Bernard Thorpe & Partners.

Andrew Huntley of Richard Ellis emphasised the problem of surplus in his article in *Estates Gazette*[1] of January 1983 and he highlighted another aspect of development: the construction industry. Huntley said: "The industrial market saw increasing amounts of old and new space coming on to the market in many areas as a result of the manufacturing industry's continuing shake-out. The devastating effects of the recession on manufacturing output in investment were illustrated by an estimated 12% fall in the value of orders for new industrial building construction in 1982."

(b) Offices

Information on the office property market is readily available, especially in the London area. Several well-established practices publish reviews for the city on a regular basis. Richard Saunders & Partners[3] report that at January 1983 7.5m sq ft of office space was available in the central area of London, and St Quintin noted in their office floorspace survey of 1981[4] that 30m sq ft of office stock was recorded in the GLC area — an increase of 30% since 1971. St Quintin also made a very valid point when they added: "It appears that the increase in the supply of office space may be more sensitive to the overall economic environment than thought hitherto". This is extremely relevant in understanding the effect of the current business environment on companies.

The office property survey of September 1982 by Bernard Thorpe & Partners[5] goes as far as quoting rents achieved on offices in London and Birmingham. In the London Borough of Holborn, Thorpes say that, there was an oversupply with many modern air-conditioned offices standing empty. Some lettings had been obtained with agreed rents at "considerably less than the £18 per sq ft which was initially quoted" — again, a problem of oversupply and slack demand forcing rents down. Top quality central area office accommodation was still in short supply in 1982 and Thorpes could sense "consumers slowly realizing the opportunities available within very easy reach of the city and interest is being shown in buildings which have remained unlet for months".

In Birmingham, Thorpes reported that demand for modern prime area offices actually exceeded supply (unlike the very depressed industrial property market in the area) and rents were expected to achieve £10 per sq ft in the spring of 1983. There was a sting in the tail for investors, however, with Thorpes stating quite clearly that, apart from these prime developments, vacant office accommodation was of the wrong size, in the wrong place and of insufficient calibre to attract takers.

Richard Ellis partner Andrew Huntley mentions increasing

caution during 1982 by institutional buyers dealing in office investment. Although central London offices remained in demand, the renewed interest in relocation, oversupply and "the implications of the new communications and microchip technology" were making investors more careful in selecting schemes. In their review of UK property in 1982[6] Richard Ellis emphasise the point, noting that "a number of companies also began to investigate the cost savings to be gained by decentralising their management functions".

Further on in their review, however, Ellis make a very valid observation about the merits of decentralisation: "There is evidence that some of the larger companies which have moved out of London are now questioning some of the basic assumptions that caused them to move". Enough said at this point, but there are clearly tremendous implications for the property marketing man in these expert observations.

Outside London, as one would expect, office accommodation is not as significant as industrial in terms of both availability and demand. The DOE estimated that in 1980 there was an office space stock of 43m sq ft in England, an increase of 15% since 1975. The average size of a single hereditament was small, about 2,700 sq ft, and around 175,000 hereditaments were involved in total. No estimate of the number that are currently vacant was available at the time of writing.

(c) Retail premises

The retail property market is currently affected by continuing rationalisation by most trading multiples. This trend has been in evidence for the last two years, according to Ron Presley of Edward Erdman in the *Estates Gazette* property review[1]. More prime shop units came on to the market in 1982 but, he notes, takers were slow to come forward. "For the first time in several years the high streets of even the more prosperous South-East towns saw units vacant for many months: estate agents' boards have appeared in high streets where they were never seen in the past". DOE statistics show only a small increase in conventional retail premises from 1975 to 1980.

In his article "Retail location through the 1980s" in the *Estates Gazette* November 13 1982, John Ratcliffe reports that between 1965 and 1980 some 424 individual retail developments of over 50,000 sq ft were undertaken, producing 65m sq ft of floorspace. He continues: "Although this volume of space is unlikely to be reproduced in a similar period, the same number of schemes could well be undertaken". Average scheme size will, however, reduce, according to Ratcliffe. It had already fallen from 232,000 sq ft in 1977 to 137,000 sq ft in 1981.

Amazingly, the total amount of new retail space created in 1981 was the highest since 1976, over 4.5m sq ft. Active interest by developers and institutions continues in the retail property market despite the prevailing economic circumstances. Perhaps it is felt that consumer spending, being an indicator of manufacturing company fortunes, can be rapidly influenced by short-term political and economic measures designed to stimulate the economy.

3.2 The consumers of property

Marketing is all about the consumer and his needs. In the previous section, among all the statistics and opinions, the consumer wanders like an anonymous entity without personality or form. Very few of the reviews that I have read suggest that the consumer as a person, or group of persons, is the single most important element in the property business. In his perspective of the 1983 property market[7] Michael Baylis, senior partner of Richard Ellis, sums up the situation succinctly. Referring to 1982 as a bad year, he says: "In such difficult times it becomes apparent that it is the occupier and his requirements that are of paramount importance to the property industry". He goes on to put developers and investors clearly in perspective. "Without the occupier and his ability to provide a return by way of rent, the investor and the developer have no function" — an excellent definition of property marketing and another reason for a professional practice to review its purpose and goals.

The aim of this short section is to make the student surveyor/valuer or the established practitioner more aware of the current business environment affecting both the manufacturing or service company and hence the demand for property.

It can be said that today's industry is in a shifting and aggressive environment, which for our purpose is examined under five main headings.

(1) Post industrial society. Dominated by the growth of the service sector, manufacturing industry now accounts for only 40% of our gross national product. At the turn of the century the level was 80%. The growth of consumerism, often backed by government legislation, is another facet of today's industrial society. A third factor is the increase in government intervention into business and industrial life. Incomes and energy policies are but two areas where legislation directly affects costs and thus the competitive position of a company.

(2) Speed of change. In order to survive, advanced technology companies in particular must have flexibility built in as a sixth sense. The ability to be able to recognise the potential of a new product or invention, or a gap in the market that will be successfully filled by the

first company to produce the product and get it to a consumer, is a valuable asset. The need for flexibility affects the choice of premises. Two good examples of the speed of technological change are the camera and the transistor. The timespan between invention and mass-production of the camera was 112 years. Given that the market needed educating in respect of the "need" for amateur photography, the market for making pictures had been in evidence for hundreds of years. By comparison, the timespan between invention and full production of the transistor was three years.

(3) Greater environmental complexity. The demands of the consumer in the era of technology dictate the development of new products of such complexity that they are beyond the capacity of banker, or surveyor, to understand. Many financial institutions have responded by forming market research departments or by buying in evaluative expertise when required. It is inevitable that the growth of specialised production techniques to satisfy the markets will again affect both the choice and specification of premises.

Company structures are also increasingly complex, more and more with international connections or overseas control. For disposal of property, this has the effect of lengthening the decision time and adding to the number of persons involved. Despite claims to the contrary, experience shows that company growth and acquisition can lead to that company becoming institutionalised and bureaucratic. The demands placed upon a company are very different in the post-industrial society, which puts additional strain upon resources and management.

The last 10 years has also seen the growth of environmentalism as an influence on modern industry. Environmentalists are obviously concerned with the protection of the environment and its resources and, while acknowledging the benefits of a thriving capitalist structure, are against the exploitation of the environment by organised business. Government legislation has been introduced to help in this respect.

(4) More turbulent environment. The effect of an unpredictable business environment is that it creates "shocks" when least expected. A classic example must be the four-fold increase in the price of oil between 1973 and 1975. The costs and shortages of raw material supplies generally can be a problem for a wide range of industries, especially where civil strife or military action elsewhere in the world affect both commodity prices and international currency levels.

The "industrial north", as Edward Heath describes it, has partly responded by switching to non-dependent manufacturing operations, thus leaving the traditional mass-production of basic goods to the new developing countries such as Taiwan, Korea and

African states. The phenomenal growth of competition from these countries is another factor influencing the development of United Kingdom industry.

(5) Slow-growth economy. Europe as a whole is suffering the effects of world recession and seems committed to an annual slow-growth economy at about the 1% to $2\frac{1}{2}$% level. An upturn in the economy of the United States seems imminent, with a 1983-84 forecast of $2\frac{1}{2}$% growth. The implications for property marketing are substantial. Inflation in the UK is currently at a low level but, even with the relatively cheap cost of borrowing, many companies are reluctant to speculate. Advanced technology firms are especially vulnerable to changes in the domestic economy, as they invariably require substantial investments for research and development programmes.

Many of the above factors and their implications on potential customers are not fully appreciated by the surveyor or valuer in his understanding of the market. A sharper interpretation of the various sectors of the market is needed with a sympathetic appreciation of the problems affecting modern management.

3.3 Demand

Although a great deal of data is available on stocks of floorspace of all types in the United Kingdom, I have found little information on lettings or sales during my research. There may be good reasons for this — client confidentiality being one, together with the perfectly acceptable commercial doctrine that, as an agent, one does not make information available to one's competitors. In addition, the sheer task of compiling the data would prove daunting, even for a government department, and if it were done many would question the value of the figures collected. For a marketing man, market information of this kind, although historical, is invaluable in assessing a company's position and strength in the market place.

In order to obtain at least a broad idea of take-up of space nationally in such a fragmented market as property, it should be possible to use published statistics of new and existing stock. Also, the views of the market by established practices give a "feel" for what is happening. The significance of not knowing enough about consumer demand was neatly summed up by Peter McManus, chairman of Property World in his report on the 1982 housing market in *Estates Gazette*[1]. Referring to factors affecting the failure of 1982 to produce a boom he says: "One answer is that no one had accurately calculated the oversupply of property".

Before examining ways in which future demand can be assessed and sales forecast, a word about the nature of property demand and supply seems appropriate. Most property developers would agree that the single most important factor affecting the supply of premises is planning regulations. Given that the supply of land is fixed, the various physical or environmental limitations on its use are overshadowed by planning policy.

The exercising of local planning authority powers in respect of allocation of land for development, intensity of development and restrictions on changes of use are not motivated by consumer demand in a marketing sense. Thus to a certain extent, the property marketers are faced with a situation that is anathema to their profession — fitting a consumer to a product, or "product orientation". Nevertheless, the style, design and price of the product may not be determined by the planning authority and in such cases the developer or agent can adopt marketing principles albeit from a relatively fixed position.

The United States' approach to this situation is to evaluate the potential of a zoned allocation with an economic development team that has a property marketing specialist as one of its key members. This ensures that the evaluation of market demand and of potential sales are undertaken at the same time as the geotechnical experts are carrying out site investigations.

Other factors affecting demand are legislation, such as the Rent Acts, and changes in the composition, age or desires of the population. For industrial and commercial property, population characteristics are of lesser importance than production techniques and resource management, but fashion will affect the style of demand for office space. Open-plan, once fashionable, has recently changed to movable, sound-restrictive partitioning such as that being marketed by Herman Miller described as the "action-office".

In boom times, the study and analysis of demand seems unimportant to the developer or agent — the principle being that wherever and whatever you build will let or sell eventually. Office developments in our capital city centres are still conceived on this basis, especially on prime sites. However, while developments remain unlet, someone has to pay the interest.

When demand is low, prices fall as each agent and developer chases an ever-decreasing and more selective market. A reduction in the supply of buildings, which would keep prices high, can really be achieved only be demolition or change of use.

The clear lesson from this argument is that the marketing surveyor or valuer who understands the changing nature of demand, and intends to monitor the variables which influence it, will be better placed when it comes to disposal of premises or recommending investments to his clients. The mistake would be to adopt a complacent attitude during boom times, as this is the very period when demand information is available to utilise when times are bad.

In the February 1983 issue of the magazine *Urban Land*, the Urban Land Institute of the United States published an article on supply and demand in the housing market. The diagram which illustrates the problem for a developer is shown in Figure 5. All markets tend to go through this "double-bell" curve, including industrial and commercial property markets, and one can plot a separate set of curves for each sector of each market.

Both the demand and supply curves are affected by all the factors discussed in this chapter so far, but typically a point occurs at which supply will start to exceed demand. If a developer is still building for this market and is unable to stimulate demand or increase his market share then he will lose, unless he can switch to another segment which is showing increasing demand. The marketer's job in the developer's company would be to forewarn the management of these changes in demand and recommend remedial action.

The article in *Urban Land* referred to an actual case where a major developer almost fell into the trap of building and selling houses in a dying market segment. However, expert marketing advice was

Fig. 5. Supply/Demand Curve (Typical 3-8 Year Cycle)

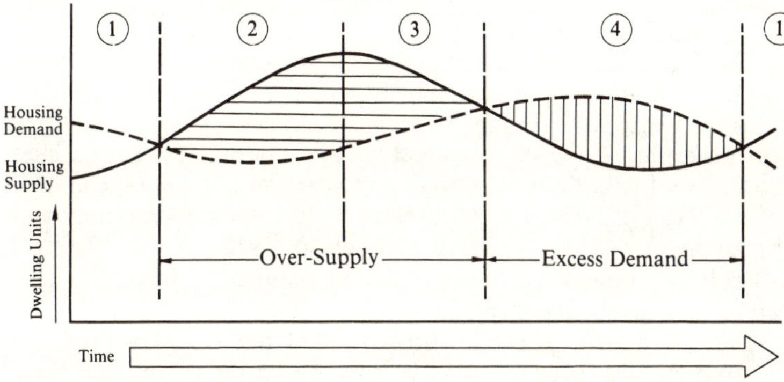

Source: Urban Land Institute

1. Demand appears high. Supply is steadily increasing to catch up. Demand is actually decreasing or leveling off while supply is starting to grow.
2. Supply is now really growing, everyone is on the bandwagon. Demand has levelled off and overbuilding is now in full swing.
3. The market is now overbuilt and construction is being cut back, but it will take some time for those who were building late in Phase 2 to sell off their inventory and work out of their excessive land holdings.
4. Demand has now exceeded supply again, but construction is still low because of previous bad experience. Construction only starts to pick up when the pent-up demand is so big it cannot be ignored.

commissioned before committing further expenditure, and the recommendations enabled the developer to diversify to fill a market gap in the same location with a new project. As the article says: "If a qualified professional (marketer) had come from outside earlier on, and given this developer a better sense of how the market was changing, the project could probably have proceeded much sooner". That time-lag represented an unnecessary high risk period for the developer.

3.4. Estimating current demand

Kotler identifies two types of estimate in which a seller (agency practice) should be interested — total market potential and territorial potential. Having established market potential, it is a senior management decision as to how much of that market the practice or company can gain and how much effort is to be made gaining it.

Total market potential is the maximum amount of sales that might be available to all competing firms during a given period in a given market segment under a given level of marketing effort and given environmental conditions. The seller wants to know if the market is large enough to justify his company's participation.

A common formula for this estimate is:
$$Q = N \times Q \times P$$
Where:
    Q = Total market potential;
    N = Number of buyers in the specific market;
    Q = Quantity purchased by an average buyer;
    P = Price of average product;

For example, if 2,000 high-technology companies buy a new production facility building every five years and the average price is £150,000 for an average 5,000 sq ft, then the total market potential is approximately £30m over a five-year period. As Kotler says, the most difficult component to measure is the number of buyers in that market in a given time period.

A variation on the formula above is called the "Chain method". It is based on the premise that it may be easier to look at each component of the magnitude rather than the magnitude itself. In the sense of property marketing an example might be that:

Current demand for high-tech buildings = { High-tech companies in UK × Average percentage of those without spare capacity on site × Average percentage of those companies who need specialised premises × Average percentage of those companies who would pay current market rent for high-tech buildings.

Once total market potential is established it must be compared with actual market size, which will always be less than market potential, before appropriate action is decided. This must not be confused with the oversupply of premises deemed to be suitable for high-tech industries: the concern here is with products rather than with markets.

The remaining factor is the company's or practice's market share and its ability to physically increase that share if so intended. A practice's market is that to which the products or services are available, accessible and attractive. To increase share, a practice can decide, if it has the capability, to attack a competitor's share or to go after the untapped market potential.

Territorial potentials are particularly attractive to commercial and industrial agents because of the traditionally "local" nature of business operations. Most property practices seem to favour a territorial approach to growth usually attained by opening offices in towns within a region rather than by expanding the head office to cover the same area.

The "market build-up" method of estimating current demand in a territory uses a classification approach based on Standard Industrial Classifications (SIC). The data enables the researcher to select target industrial groups and relate these to the number of establishments in a territory together with their buying potential, which may be based upon profits or turnover. Market potential can then be assessed for that particular target group. If the same method is used for other territories then the practice can decide how much marketing effort and budget should be allocated to that territory for an attack on that particular market.

Major consumer companies have had considerable difficulty in establishing territorial potential among the general public. Until recently, no reliable method had been devised for classifying households in the same way as industries. The development of the ACORN system in the United Kingdom by CACI now enables consumer companies to classify spending power based on housing type in the given territory. Prior to this, marketers used simple index systems based on populations and information gathered by surveys. These were based mainly on local authority administrative areas or television regions rather than target market areas. Adaptation of the ACORN system by the residential agency practice could prove to be very valuable in estimating market potential in the territory and in providing a focus for promotion.

3.5. Estimating future demand

The science of forecasting future demand has now become very sophisticated. Demand forecasting is the raw material of marketing planning and is a dangerous area. Philip Kotler sums it up well when he says: "Forecasting is hard, particularly of the future".

Kotler identifies six major methods of forecasting which are based on three simple parameters: what people say, what people do and what people have done. I have adapted the six methods for the surveyor and valuer as follows:

(a) What people say
(i) Surveys of buyer intentions. The use of marketing research techniques is covered in depth in Chapter 6: at this point it is sufficient to say that in the property industry it is possible to survey not only buyer intentions but a great deal more besides. There are advantages for commercial agents over mass consumer marketers in that buyers are relatively few, it can be cost-effective to reach them and they usually have clear intentions which they will carry out given the right environmental conditions. I believe it is also possible to establish buyer intentions in the residential market by the use of modern research techniques.

(ii) Composite of sales-force opinion. Especially valuable if opinion is based upon real field experience although this may be territorially based, rather than regional or national. My research indicates that surveyors based in London have limited knowledge of demand at a national level, depending for information instead upon their regional offices. Unfortunately, their interpretation of regional reports is conditioned by their personal field experience, which is limited to the capital.

Sales-force opinion is generally biased although full of detailed local knowledge. There is a natural tendency for salesmen to over- or under-estimate the potential future demand of their area. Nevertheless, the aggregated opinions are valuable, in providing an estimate of demand.

(iii) Expert opinion. Not only very useful to the marketer but usually free, expert opinion can be obtained simply by talking to those involved in property development and marketing. Architects, development companies and funding institutions spring to mind as obvious examples. Many industrial companies buy in expert opinion from acknowledged experts who may act in a consultant capacity. It must be remembered, however, that individual expert opinions *are* opinions and not fact.

(b) What people do
This can best be measured by what is termed a "Test-market method", which literally means placing the product into a selected market territory for consumers to use. This is done in a variety of ways depending upon development costs, research costs and, of

course, timing. The research team will be looking for feedback in the form of initial sales, frequency of purchase and consumer opinion.

The method is, however, rather inapplicable to expensive industrial products (an extreme example of which would be Concorde) where producing a few samples for test-marketing would be costly and difficult. Industrial companies have to use alternative methods and these may include trade shows (Farnborough Air Show) dealers' rooms (BL's outlets) or controlled test-marketing (a sample made by a sub-contractor and sold in a selected geographic location by a third-party).

What about the factory, office or shop? None lend themselves to test-marketing very easily. I believe that the answer lies in using the method in reverse, by bringing the consumer to the product in the case of speculative development or by taking a facsimile of the product to the consumer. In both cases, I am talking about test-marketing *not* a presentation of the finished development, which is a promotional activity unconnected with forecasting demand.

(c) What people have done

(i) Time-series analysis. This method attempts to forecast demand based upon past causal relationships that are uncovered through analysis. But danger exists in a mechanical extrapolation of what appear to be trends without a realistic assessment of what might happen tomorrow. Environmental "shocks", discussed previously, have a nasty habit of upsetting time-series analyses.

There are causal relationships between company sales, the cost of borrowing and the demand for new industrial or commercial floorspace. The problem in analysis may be in assimilating the data on past purchase activity.

(ii) Statistical-demand analysis. Unlike time-series analysis, this method does not use sales as a function of time but as a function of other underlying variables such as prices, income and population. It is particularly appropriate for markets which are not stable over time.

3.6. Implications for the surveyor

To summarise this chapter, what are the implications for the surveyor or valuer involved in property? Clearly, the oversupply of property, even allowing for that which is obsolete, together with the more sophisticated selectivity by the ever-diminishing buyer market, means that only the best practices will survive profitably in agency work.

There is a need for the practice to utilise demand measurement techniques in order to take on the competition. As Peter McManus warns in referring to the domination of the housing market by a few building giants, "more and more buyers will enter the market via a new home, bypassing the estate agent completely". The underlying intentions of Lloyds Bank in setting up Black Horse Agencies are also patently obvious, although denied, in that the attraction of taking a large portion of the estate agency market in the United Kingdom must be strong. Lloyds have both the money and enough marketing expertise, including demand analysis, to put into their estate agency practice to have a potentially devastating effect. In addition, the activities of the other banks in this and the commercial markets should not be ignored.

I believe that these infringements of the professional surveyor's work in residential practice will soon creep into commercial practice. The traditional activity of speculative building for a market that has never been researched properly and where the approach has been product orientated, seems inappropriate and even foolhardy in the present circumstances. Experts do not seem to believe any more that property will eventually let, given the right price and sufficient time.

A major consideration in today's market, and an important source of business for the professional practice, are the investment institutions. They too are currently rationalising their portfolios and investing money elsewhere. Paul Orchard-Lisle of Healey & Baker, in his investment market report in *Estates Gazette* of January 1983, claims that investment institutions are unable to invest all the funds they allocate to property investment. A shortfall of £1bn each year has been estimated. In the same issue, Andrew Huntley of Richard Ellis says: "Investment funding in 1982 was also inhibited by the lack of new, well-located quality developments". But one of the key statements comes in Richard Ellis' UK property report. Under the heading "A new direction in property marketing," it says: "The major problem is that developers and institutions undertaking development are not responding to true tenant demand, but constructing buildings based upon historic, rather than current, requirements."

3.7. The future market

That things are going to change seems without doubt, but it is not my function to forecast changes in demand or trends in the property market place. It is, however, rewarding to take the composite view of expert opinion. I have listed below a number of significant expert opinions expressed this year which, when taken together, probably represent a pretty good estimate of what will happen over the next 12 months.

Industrial property

"The bright hope for the industrial market has been the growth of high-technology industries." — Derek Penfold, news editor of *Estates Gazette*[7].

"Buildings and their environment are designed to cater both for their product and for the people who work in them. Modern industry has requirements from both points of view." — Property and Technology report, Herring Son & Daw[8].

"Our main competitor [for overseas projects], West Germany, is well placed to offer a strong package with excellent infrastructure and technical resources." (ibid.)

"There is very little evidence to suggest an imminent recovery in either output or investment by manufacturing industry." (Obviously seen as a variable component affecting demand by the writer.) — United Kingdom Property Report 1983, Richard Ellis[6].

"The recession has reduced profit margins and has made the job of anticipating market demand more difficult." — William Mitchell, president of the National Association of Industrial and Office Parks, USA[9].

Commercial property

"In analysing the future investment potential of the commercial property market, it is imperative that well-researched demand and supply statistics are studied." — Andrew Huntley, Richard Ellis.

"This year (1982) will see further rationalisation before the economy provides sufficient impetus to promote expansion in retail growth." — Ron Presley, Edward Erdman.

"The continuing excess of supply over demand will temper prospects for rental growth in the short term." — Andrew Huntley, Richard Ellis.

"An increase in consumer spending will stimulate demand for [retail] accommodation." — Property Market Survey 1983, St Quintins[10].

"New trends in information technology will affect the market for office property in several major respects." — *Property and information technology*, College of Estate Management research report[11].

"Some [investment] funds may adopt a more venturesome approach to secondary property where good management and marketing could realise higher returns than those available from absolute prime positions." — John Ratcliffe, Polytechnic of the South Bank[12].

No really clear message comes through from these quotes, other than that there will be challenges for the property profession in the future market. Lack of buoyancy will call for flair and innovation; high-technology growth will need sound research to establish user-requirements, and the challenge from the rest of Europe will demand competitive action. All these key activities can be in the armoury of the modern marketing surveyor.

References. Chapter 3.

[1] 1982 Property Review. Estates Gazette. January 22nd 1983.
[2] 1982 Industrial Floorspace Survey. Bernard Thorpe & Partners.
[3] 1983. Office Review. Richard Saunders & Partners.
[4] 1981. Office Floorspace Survey. St. Quintins.
[5] 1982. Office Property Survey. Bernard Thorpe & Partners.
[6] United Kingdom Property Report 1983. Richard Ellis. January 1983.
[7] "Urban Land" February 1983. Urban Land Institute. (USA)
[8] "Property & Technology — The Needs of Modern Industry." Herring Son & Daw. 1982.
[9] William Mitchell. Carter and Associates. Atlanta, Georgia. Business Facilities. February 1983.
[10] 1983 Property Market Survey. St. Quintins.
[11] "Property and Information Technology." Centre for Advanced Land Use Studies 1982.
[12] "Retail location through the 1980s" John Ratcliffe. Estates Gazette. November 13th 1982.

CHAPTER 4
The Product

When considering the product in the context of professional practice, it is appropriate to remember that the definition of marketing clearly identifies "consumer requirements", meaning a need of a consumer or group of consumers. The need can obviously be for advice, problem-solving, specialist skills such as dentistry, as well as for material products or goods. It is the understanding of this need, with all its implications for growth and success, that would seem to give the chartered surveyor so much difficulty.

Nigel Stephens covers this aspect in *The Practice of Estate Agency*[1] and, perhaps without realising it, falls into the trap of viewing the "product" for a residential agency as being only a residential property. However, he quite rightly points out that in order to attract instructions from customers, the agency must present itself to the market place once it has established an office in a new area. In other words, the practice must market *itself* in order to fulfil its profit objectives.

Chapter 5 contains my views on how the practice can market itself, because I am attempting to differentiate between the needs and expectations of the consumer in respect of both expert services and the disposal of property and the way in which the practice is marketed as a credible entity in the market place.

The "product", then, in marketing terms consists of three aspects:

(a) Expert services;
(b) Property disposal (where the product could be described more aptly as a building or site);
(c) The practice.

I shall deal with the first two in this chapter and the third in Chapter 5.

4.1. The buyers

Derek Penfold's prologue in the *Estates Gazette* review of 1982 had a strong message for those involved in the provision of expert advice on property investments. Referring to the conditions of 1982 dictating that agents had to work harder for their fees, he says: "Many institutions it is said, long attached to a firm for investment advice, are shopping around for new advisers." A complacent view of existing clients would, Penfold suggests, be very dangerous. His advice is particularly appropriate for this chapter: "Firms have got to be more on the ball than some may have been with the previous security of in-house investment clients".

Clearly then, investment institutions are beginning to review the performance of their expert advisers more critically — a natural reaction in economically depressed times. The institutions are not only reducing their investment portfolio in property but are also perhaps critically assessing the role of the surveyor and his ability to identify and to let prime investments.

There is strong evidence to suggest that investors could benefit in the medium to long term from the growth prospects of high-technology industries. It is the professional adviser who must lead the investor to this potential market. Herring Son & Daw in their report *Property and Technology*[2], advise that investors should "put their money in the property where the modern demand lies rather than persist in seeking the apparent safety of mature or even declining occupational patterns".

It is the investment surveyor or valuer who puts together the high-technology development package for the institution, using his knowledge of the industry and its requirements through his marketing research activities. He prepares a marketing campaign for the development covering every aspect of product promotion. He describes how the property is to be let, under what conditions and he puts together an impressive professional presentation for his client.

Companies giving instructions to a commercial agent for disposal of property will, like institutional investors, invariably come into contact with the experienced chartered surveyor or valuer. Unlike the institution, however, many company directors may have had little or no experience of property practices other than in the sale and purchase of their own homes. What do they expect?

Few would argue with the expert valuation of the premises as a prerequisite to its disposal, but when it comes to a so-called "marketing campaign" proposed by the agent, senior management is becoming more and more sceptical. It is important to remember that the responsibility for property disposal within an industrial company may well rest with the marketing man rather than the accountant. Many senior directors have also had considerable marketing experience in their respective fields and it will take them no time at all to see through a surveyor who attempts to convince them that the main thrust of his proposed campaign centres around extensive advertising in the press, paid for by the company, not the agent.

As with institutions, therefore, what is required is much greater concentration on the satisfying of consumer requirements. I accept that, as far as the agent is concerned, the "buyer" of expert services and skills is the company that issued the instructions, not the potential buyer of the property in question. Having said that, I am very conscious of the fact that all potential buyers are customers of the agent as well; there is no conflict in this as far as marketing is concerned. Much has yet to be done in the profession with regard to the treatment of potential clients.

It is in this category of service that costs become a sensitive and much-debated issue. Companies with a long tradition of manufacturing are usually extremely expert at pricing goods but not services. Few would appreciate that maintaining a modest office with qualified staff, whose work will cover salaries and overheads as well as contribute to the profits of the practice, means charging the kind of fees that agents agree with clients. The problem is exacerbated by the fact that agents also expect clients to pay for all promotional activity — advertising, literature and so on.

Companies fully understand the agreement of no sale, no fee, but when property *is* let or sold the fee is invariably a big one. Add to this the fact that firms wishing to dispose of property are unable or unwilling to do it themselves and feel that they have no choice but to seek the services of a commercial agent and one can see why criticism and frustration starts to creep in. In my own experience as a management consultant, a daily rate for expert advice in 1980 was negotiable around £150-£300 exclusive, depending upon the nature of the job and the length of the contract. Industrial clients, again usually marketing or managing directors, would agree to an all-inclusive fixed-price fee for the whole job in advance. The two great advantages to the company of this system are that several consultants can be asked to submit proposals on a tender basis, and that the client knows in advance what his cash outlay will be within a given time-period.

While I appreciate that commercial agents are nowadays more frequently asked to submit schemes for the disposal of premises, few do so with detailed costs or a realistic timescale on a competitive basis with other agents. It may be impractical from the agent's point of view to do this because he never really has control over the timescale within which a property will be sold. There are, however, no uncertainties or restrictions to the fees that would be charged or other services that the agency may be able to provide to ensure that the client is satisfied with performance and progress.

The problem for the company is that although payment can be made for the surveyor's other expert services, and these are both real and predictable within an agreed timescale, arrangements for property disposal are so loose that the firm tends to give less attention to the problem than to any special services provided for it by other experts. The involvement is often no more than the occasional progress meeting and authorisation of invoices for promotional charges.

If an agent fails to dispose of the property within a time-period imposed by the client, rather than by the market, then he can find himself being dismissed or joined by one or more other agents. Neither procedure seems satisfactory, and as a marketer I am convinced that there must be another way, which commits both client and agent to a mutually-acceptable programme containing time and budget constraints.

My objective in this chapter is not to become involved in a discussion on agents' fees, or sole and multiple agency practices. However, as a recent newcomer to the property world from a different discipline, I am able to describe a view held by businesses outside the profession. I hope that this will be valuable in forcing a change of direction.

Perhaps the answer is the value for money perceived by the client. This has much to do with the style of the agent's practice and the way in which the client is treated by the individual staff. More of this in Chapter 5.

The next group of consumers to whom the property practice must pay heed are the potential buyers. In boom times, when supply is exceeded by demand, buyers can be treated rather disdainfully by agents. During times of recession, the few buyers that do exist are not really nursed by agents except that they may receive more mailshots than usual.

Buyers fall into three main categories. Those who have an immediate need, those who want to be kept informed because they may have a need in the future and those who have no real need but may be persuaded to buy, given the right deal in the right location. Although this last group may be difficult to find, it should not be difficult for the marketing-orientated surveyor, valuer or practice to attempt to undertake the search. The problem is that this potential market is constantly changing as companies move and deals are agreed. Market research on a monitoring basis, is the answer, and this will be covered in Chapter 6.

The surveyor must be able to distinguish between the three categories of buyers because the approach to each is different. What must also be understood is why consumers want to buy. For expert services such as property portfolio management, structural surveys, rating valuations or investment appraisals, the answer is generally obvious but for the purchase of premises I have turned to the book *Modern Methods of Valuation* by Britton, Davies and Johnson[3]. The authors put forward three buying reasons in property: (a) The purchaser wishes to occupy the property to derive the economic and commercial benefit; (b) The purchaser wishes to regard the property as an investment yielding an annual income; and (c) The purchaser wishes to buy the premises and re-sell at a higher price to make a capital gain. The surveyor or valuer is definitely involved in each of these objectives, which themselves are obviously not mutually exclusive.

Each buying group may have any one or more of the three reasons for wanting to buy. The first group must of course be given absolute priority, especially during the present economic climate. Cultivation and attention are the key elements here, together with a real understanding of the buyer's needs, problems and, most importantly, his expectations of the service he will receive from the practice. None of these buyers will pay a fee to the agent and the agent must respect the wishes of his client. This should not affect the way in which a buyer is treated by the agency, yet how often do we hear of a shoddy performance in this vital area.

The second buying group needs long-term cultivation and provides a marvellous opportunity, so often overlooked, for the surveyor to establish himself in the commercial lifestyle of that buyer. I accept that long-term cultivation of this buying group can be expensive, but can the practices who hold this view confess that they have evaluated all their other promotional activities? Are they really marketing themselves? Are all the partners in the practice committed to obtaining more business?

The final buying group demands a more sophisticated approach, for which the practice requires a good marketing intelligence service and a trained sales team. In Chapter 6 I hope to explain how market research can be used to further this end and how to turn the research findings into action. To date, identification of dormant demand of this kind has been left to chance, stimulation being effected by such things as a random mailshot.

In summary then, several groups of consumers form the buying market for the professional practice and these can be sub-divided into smaller groups by nature of demand and specific needs.

Further sub-division is possible by an analysis of buying reasons or objectives. This method of segmentation allows a better understanding of those who provide the surveyor's livelihood and enables the practice to make the optimum allocation of resources. The "product" of the practice is the provision of expert advice on a range of property matters for which a fee is received from somebody. This is more than sufficient justification for each practice to review its advisory activities to ensure that the best possible service is being provided at a competitive cost.

4.2. The property life-cycle

In this section I want to consider the "product" as being the property and the way in which it can be evaluated, changed and presented to the market place. I will also cover product life-cycles and the recent impact of high-technology industrial developments

Michael Baylis, in the 1983 Property Report by Richard Ellis[4], says: "Occupiers' needs are changing very rapidly with fundamental changes in the type of premises required, a demand for new standards of design and finish". This represents a significant recognition of the fact that traditional industrial premises may no longer be suitable for those companies who are currently growing rather than declining. Marketers will not forget, however, that markets are dynamic, not static, and today's growth may be tomorrow's decline.

"The bright hope for the industrial market and indeed for the country has been the growth of high-technology industries," states Derek Penfold in the *Estates Gazette* of January 1983[5], "but the property market was slow to appreciate the special needs of this type of occupier." So there appears to be a consumer demand for special buildings to which the industry has been slow to respond. Why is this?

The good marketer would have anticipated demand much earlier and ensured that the product was available at the right price when the demand came. It must have fallen to the surveyor, as the property expert, to fulfil this role and yet it seems that this was not achieved. Three main factors may have accounted for this apparent slow response.

First, few investing institutions have been prepared to invest funds in high-technology developments, preferring to leave this to development authorities and concentrating instead on office and retail schemes with traditional industrial projects in prime and secondary locations. This lack of investment interest is partly due to the out-dated use classes under current planning regulations and to restrictions on office space for industrial building allowances. The fault must also lie to a large extent with the investing institutions in their reluctance to accept new designs, innovative schemes and more flexible leases.

Secondly, the surveying profession is not familiar with the uses and techniques of market research and therefore was unable to foresee demand, let alone estimate the size of the market, what it comprised and what "products" were required. I do not believe that these matters, vital to the property profession, should be left to architects or quantity surveyors. It is the surveyor who should be most in touch with the property market and it is he who must lead the other professions in understanding demand and influencing design and location.

Finally, a great deal of industrial property was, and still is, on the market, giving rise to a reluctance by both developers and investors to build any more. There is still a demand for traditional premises but this appears to be declining. As Michael Baylis says, "Technological advances are affecting the pace at which buildings become obsolescent and the ways in which offices and industrial space are utilised".

This brings us to a problem affecting all types of property, namely its useful life. In marketing terms this is referred to as the product life-cycle.

All products have a life-cycle that follows the basic pattern of introduction, growth, maturity and decline. In consumer markets the cycle usually follows the pattern shown in Figure 6: the so-called "cycle-recycle" pattern in Figure 7 occurs because of a promotional push designed to temporarily arrest decline. The product life-cycle of an industrial or commercial building may follow the scalloped pattern shown in Figure 8, where each dip in the curve coincides with a change of use of the product but the overall slope is in decline eventually leading to demolition. This need not be an economic disaster for the owners, however, as the site may be worth more money than the building, at a certain point in time.

I would suggest that separate product life-cycle curves exist for buildings which are built speculatively and those which are bespoke, in that maximum sales/profits are achieved at different times. Both types, however, become obsolete eventually, although this may take anything up to 50 years or more and, unlike a washing machine, a building cannot be disposed of easily and cheaply.

During its life a building may be marketed several times and on each occasion, except the first in the case of bespoke projects, it will never exactly suit the requirements of the new user. Part of the reason for this is that the introduction of new technology in production methods is happening at a faster pace than the design, construction,

Fig. 6 Product life cycle. Normal pattern

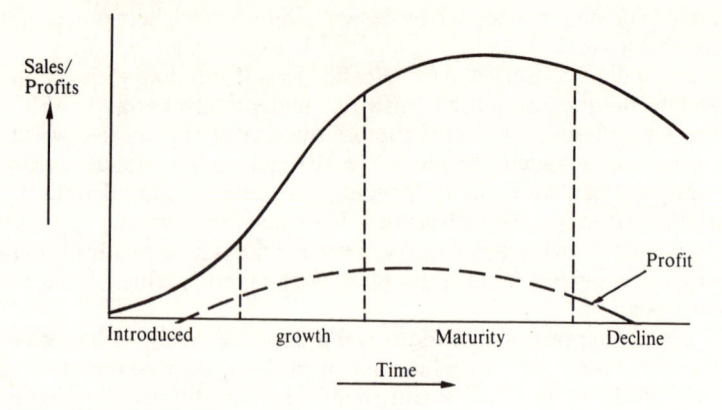

Fig. 7 Product life cycle. "Cycle-recycle" pattern

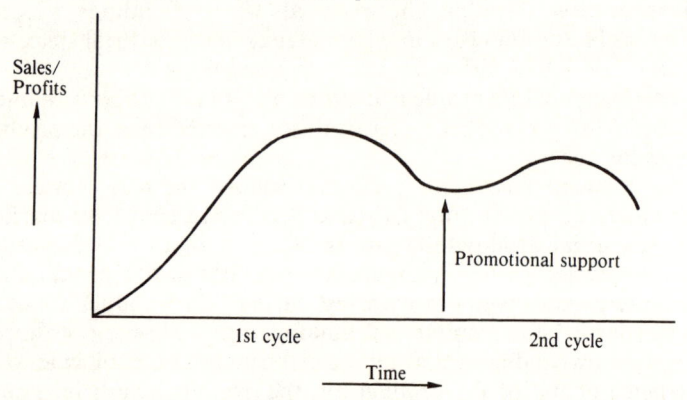

Fig. 8 Product life cycle. Property pattern

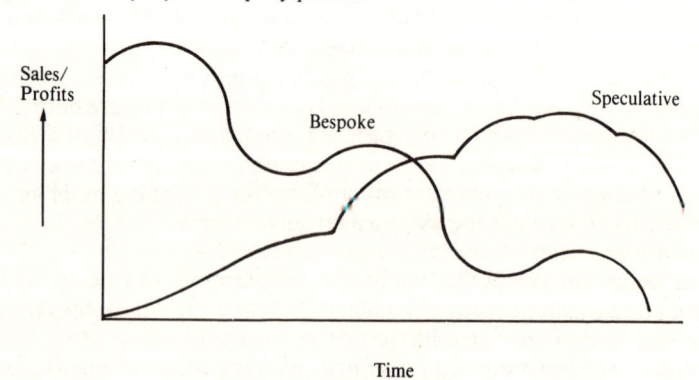

occupation and demolition of buildings. Furthermore, consumer and industrial markets are themselves changing rapidly, so that the surveyor is faced with a double-edged problem. Firstly, the building he is trying to let or sell may be unsuitable for the application of new technology to the industry for which the unit was originally designed; and secondly, that particular industry may be in a declining market where the products are no longer required. The steel industry would be a good example.

This, of course, explains the investment institutions' insistence on an all-purpose flexible development scheme where several industries and uses can be accommodated by the same buildings.

Any property will also deteriorate with time, unless very well maintained, thus affecting rents and therefore by definition appealing to several different sectors of the market during its useful life. A further complication is that the style and design of the average building is unlikely to be cost-effectively adaptable to the ever-changing, often fashionable, demands of the market.

In Figure 9 I have attempted to describe the stages of a typical industrial building through its life-cycle. At each stage a different sector of the market is involved with different needs. This in turn dictates a change in the product, such as in its appearance or fittings and, more importantly, in the way it is presented to a particular buyer group or target market.

4.3. Presentation of premises

Many surveyors claim that the appearance of the premises is not important since most industrialists expect new premises to have landscaping still in progress on the site and second-hand premises to be showing signs of wear and tear. I believe this view to be as false as that held by consumers who claim to be unaffected by advertising. Of course we are affected by both appearances and images. The presentation of an industrial building, office or shop, by whatever means, is not just a matter of information or an indication of the level of maintenance undertaken by the previous occupant: it is a reflection of the letting agent's professional skill in judging the requirements, image and status of the potential buyer.

The agent is also saying something about his own professionalism in the way he presents premises to the market. If this were not true, then major consumer companies would not spend so much money on advertising, multi-national industrial groups would not concern themselves with corporate image-building, the sales team would not have good-quality company cars and 50% of the population would not wear digital watches. All this proccupation with images and status is real and is a fundamental component of our society.

Market Sector	Status	Lessee/owner	Value
Buoyant/innovative new technologies	Premises new (spec. or bespoke)	Growth industry	High
↓	↓	↓	↓
Buoyant/ static established companies	Premises second-hand	Traditional industry	Medium
↓	↓	↓	↓
Static/depressed	Premises third-hand part unusable	Distributive trade	Cheaper
↓	↓	↓	↓
Erratic high failure rate	Premises fourth-hand split into small units nearing end of useful life	Car-repairs storage (temporary) Railway-arch enterprise starters	Bottom-consideration given to major refurbishment or demolition

Fig. 9 The Property "Product" life cycle

Industrial and commercial premises have been the poor relation for a long time in presentational terms. The series of photographs numbered 1 to 12 show a number of speculative industrial buildings which illustrate the point. Appearances range from impressive to ordinary; there is little doubt as to which a potential buyer in a new growth market will select, with the current choice available.

What makes the presentation of premises so important is that there is evidence to suggest that the cost and location of the property may not just be the overriding factors in a purchasing decision by any of the buying groups. Experience has shown that buyers will pay a premium for premises in the right location; but is this the only reason? How does the appearance of the building influence the decision? Can decisions be influenced by professional "packaging" of the property?

Michael Baylis of Richard Ellis talks of "location, cost and timing" as being the three most critical factors affecting decisions on property purchase, rather than the old surveyor's adage of "location, location and location". The influence of cost and timing are easy to recognise and must vary from buyer to buyer. Under "location", however, I would suggest that a whole range of variable determinants are in the industrialist's mind when considering premises. The relative importance of each component will vary from company to company and will obviously be influenced by the kind of premises being sought. Nevertheless, to illustrate my point, Figure 10 sets out what I believe are the main factors influencing a buyer in the three categories of premises with which this book is concerned. The factors are grouped under the "location" heading and assume that the cost of rent and timing are considered separately.

The table shows that many factors are related directly to the actual location of the premises and as such cannot be changed or influenced by the surveyor. Again, while the marketing surveyor should ensure that he has comprehensive information on transport services, labour and suppliers, he is generally unable to influence the availability or costs of these. (I am convinced that this is not altogether true, especially in the assisted areas of the United Kingdom. In addition, more liaison with the bodies responsible for the provision of these services would also enhance development packages presented to investing institutions.) The surveyor can, however, influence or even determine the components of the proposal that are under his direct control: namely, the perception of the company as an efficient organisation by buyers and the image that the property would project if it were selected. This is what I call the corporate "feel" of the place, which will vary considerably depending upon the size, age and type of company concerned.

54 The Marketing of Industrial and Commercial Property

Fig. 10 Factors influencing the "location" decision

	Factors	Premises required		
		Industrial	Offices	Shops
Physical	Road access	✓	✓	
	Local transport facilities (4 modes)	✓		
	Costs	✓		
	Local transport infrastructure			✓
	Workforce travel pattern	✓	✓	
	Local suppliers	✓		
	Local services (telecoms, energy etc.)	✓	✓	
Identity	Development mix		✓	✓
	Town/City centre location			✓
	"Buyers" likely perception	✓	✓	
	Corporate "feel" (Image)	✓	✓	
	Location of competitors	✓	✓	✓
Sales	"Proximity" to markets	✓		
Operational	Local labour and skills	✓	✓	
	Housing for management	✓	✓	
	Local social/economic profile	✓	✓	✓
	Local cultural aspects and lifestyle	✓	✓	✓

The Product

Recent research undertaken by the Welsh Development Agency among high-technology companies showed that the majority of firms in this field considered that image as projected by premises was important. Some went so far as to suggest that external cladding materials and their colour were an integral part of image and that certain industries were connected with certain images in the minds of customers — electronics companies, for example, being linked with mirrored glass and blue and silver colours. In the survey, however, the favourite external cladding selected from a range of options offered to respondents was brick.

These growth companies are also concerned with landscaping. New estates such as the Cambridge Science Park have gone to extremes in this respect by providing a good deal of landscaping, which has great appeal to those industries who are mindful of their image in the market place.

However, there is a limit to how much a company will pay for image in terms of the structure and appearance of the premises and the immediate environment. Some may decide to spend money on renovating poor buildings, but this does not seem to happen often, possibly because of the cost and the disruption entailed. In addition, the long-term uncertainty of future profit growth mitigates against companies speculating such investment. Major international companies, on the other hand, almost invariably want to build their own premises, in which case the marketing surveyor will have presented a series of sites to the client, bearing in mind that all the factors in the table still apply.

This leaves the majority of potential buyers with the choice of new speculative developments or second-hand property, where the first question that any surveyor or valuer will ask is: "If the premises are to be 'repackaged', who is going to pay?" Of course, the answer will be the owner and he must be persuaded that an investment in the property now will pay dividends later. The surveyor's difficulty here is that because he may not be using market research to "identify and anticipate requirements" he is unable to put forward a convincing case for this further investment of money. The result is often a half-hearted "cosmetic" approach, such as a quick repaint.

I appreciate fully that many property owners are very reluctant to take this action, depending instead upon the agent's ability to find a buyer at some time in the future. For some locations this may be the most cost-effective procedure, but for the majority of premises, in a non-buoyant market, the cost of the maintenance, rates and security of empty buildings may be quite high and if prolonged could prove very costly to the owner. In addition, unless they are well maintained, the premises will deteriorate, or perhaps be vandalised, which in turn reduces both their value and their market potential.

Speed is therefore of the essence and the surveyor must produce a well-researched and feasible plan for repackaging the property prior to launching it on the market place. In the case of new speculative development the marketing surveyor should be involved from the outset as a member of the design team, where he can influence image and environment through his marketing skills.

For proposed development schemes, the institutional client will expect to see a well-thought-out and impressive document with research information, a marketing plan and evidence that design, location and costs are an accurate reflection of consumer demand. The presentation should also contain a detailed analysis of that demand and an assessment of competitive schemes.

It is true that unless a scheme follows a traditional design pattern which will appeal to the widest possible market, then the institutions may not be interested, preferring to invest funds elsewhere. The institutional market therefore needs "educating", and I am convinced that it will eventually follow the trend in the United States by responding positively to the surveyor who puts together a researched and professional development package, where all objections can be turned to advantages and which calls upon the surveyor to act as a "super-salesman". The trend has already started with the Sun Alliance Group investing in the high-technology Linford Wood development built by Milton Keynes Development Corporation.

4.4. Product pricing

The planning of product packaging cannot be undertaken without the consideration of price. It is not my intention to discuss the art (or is it a science?) of valuation of property but to make some observations on pricing and its place in marketing planning.

John Winkler, in an article on pricing strategy in the April 1983 issue of *Marketing*[6] makes the very valid point that "correct pricing is vital to the success of most companies, but strategies are often devised by accountants rather than marketing managers". Philip Kotler substantiates this unhappy situation by pointing out that the problems companies encounter in their pricing policies result from their inability to capitalise on changes in the market place and a preoccupation with the cost of producing the product rather than its selling price in the market. The major problem, however, is that prices are often set independently of the rest of the marketing mix and not as an intrinsic part of the competitive strategy.

Consumer and industrial manufacturers in volume markets are faced with a constant need to evaluate their pricing policies and objectives. Here, the activities of competitors in lucrative markets occupy much management time, and decisions are made rapidly in order to react to changes in consumer demand. In the property industry, the effects of pricing decisions are much longer term, with investors seeking rental growth from a property over a number of years.

This does not mean that price is unimportant. Demand and supply of property are, in theory, equated at any particular time to some level of price. Economic law dictates that an increase in demand or a decrease in supply of a product will result in a price increase. Conversely, a drop in demand or increase in supply will bring about a price fall. I do not believe, however, that price rations the supply and matches it to demand, as often stated in books on valuation. This may have been the case in a freely-operating buoyant market but it is not true now.

It seems that whilst new property prices bear some relation to the cost of construction they are often aligned to what price can be negotiated with a purchaser. A "market", rather than an "economic", rent is certainly being sought for speculative property in situations where subsidies are available, such as an assisted area. Elsewhere, investors quite rightly demand a return on investment and this determines not only what is built, but how much it will be offered for on the market.

In the case of second-hand property, the valuer's role is to provide an estimate of market value. According to Britton, Davies and Johnson, the valuer's estimate "will be based upon prices previously paid, but he must adjust this basis to allow for the changes since the previous transactions took place". As a marketer, I am not entirely sure how this can be achieved, since by tradition the valuer perhaps does not have access to the right kind of marketing intelligence or research data. One assumes, therefore, that price is based upon historical data and the limits set by the vendor. The question really is; what will the market pay for property? Working the market is a subtle skill and competitive edges must be kept sharp if one is to keep ahead of rivals. An approach to the establishment of what the market will bear is provided by John Winkler and I have modified this for the property profession.

Step 1.   Set price policy objectives (limits, timescale, fall-back position).
Step 2.   Identify influencing factors (presentation, location, economic factors, etc).
Step 3.   Review market information (demand, market, profile, segmentation).

Step 4.	Review competitive information (competitive schemes, empty property, activities of agents, selling prices).
Step 5.	Review costs (grants, incentives).
Step 6.	Establish pricing strategy (special offers, rent-free periods, lease-back, reverse premiums).
Step 7	Set price and negotiating level (asking price, fall-back price).
Step 8	Review price performance (regular monitoring).

In marketing terms this would be considered a systematic approach to the pricing of property. It can be seen from my notes in brackets that certain items have appeared already in previous chapters. "Presentation" under Step 2 has been dealt with in this chapter, so has "demand" listed under Step 3 and "segmentation" will be dealt with under Chapter 7.

4.5. New product development

In 1979 the Centre for Advanced Land Use Studies (CALUS) at Reading undertook a study[7] to appraise the performance of speculative industrial buildings. One finding of the study was that most private-sector developers felt that a dual-purpose (ie factory and warehouse) building was acceptable, while most public-sector developers suggested that it was not. CALUS also found that developers generally gain their knowledge "second hand from agents, designers and even from finance institutions, rather than directly from tenants".

The apparent inability of the private sector to identify and anticipate consumer demand and to exploit it allows the public sector developer to forge ahead, not because he is any more market-orientated than his colleagues in the private sector but because he is not forced to view the market in purely financial terms. Funds are available to promote developments on a wide scale and to subsidise construction costs.

There is no doubt that the biggest growth potential exists now in a number of specialised industrial sectors, such as electronics, bio-engineering, fibre-optics, organic chemicals and health-care, and what is even more exciting is the prospect of a number of these technology-based activities joining together on new projects. These industries demand more than a standard dual-use facility with the usual headroom, 10% office space etc, and this need should have been identified by the property professional years ago, as it was in the United States. Herring, Son & Daw's report[3] clearly states that "the designs of office and warehouse buildings favoured by developers and institutions are suitable only for their traditional occupiers, many of whom are drawn from the declining industries which suffer most from the new technologies. Newer industries — the area from which we look for continuing growth — want more flexible offices, very light, clean industrial space, better site layout and amenities. They also want several types of use combined in one building". That institutions are reluctant to invest in such developments is patently obvious, but their reticence must have a lot to do with the development proposals presented to them.

It seems unlikely that the developer or surveyor researches his potential market properly or puts together a professional presentation of the scheme. In fact, unlike in the USA, marketing input from a professional is nowhere to be seen in the development appraisal and presentation activity. Developers depend instead on their instincts, on an architect to design the scheme (no research data here either) and on a commercial agent to advertise the units in the property press. Is it any wonder that institutions are reluctant to speculate?

The investors are themselves perhaps now taking a lead in the reassessment of their stance towards industrial and office development, and I am encouraged by an article in the *Chartered Surveyor Weekly* of March 1983[8] in which John Parry, managing director of Commercial Union Properties, seeks to clarify the science park and high-technology estate confusion. He also encourages developers and surveyors alike to examine what makes a science park a viable investment.

Parry identifies a science park as having specialised research and development accommodation, limited manufacturing facilities, and occupiers with a close affinity to a major scientific academic faculty. In contrast, he describes a high-technology development as a glossy light-industrial/warehouse park, with better-than-average-quality buildings and occupiers, having superior layout and general amenity and with a bias towards a high office content.

What is suggested here is that two different sectors of the market would be catered for by the style and mix of speculative development. Parry goes on to identify the four most important factors that, in his view as an investor, make a successful science park:

(a) Marketability as a long-term property investment.
(b) Continuing rental growth.
(c) Lack of planning restriction on use and density.
(d) Skilled management.

Given that these criteria may be difficult to achieve, especially as the "consumer" may have very different ideas on what he needs, Parry predicts that institutions *will* invest in specialised developments and sees difficulties as only transitory. He advocates the setting-up of a special fund as an investment vehicle for the purpose.

It is clear from this article that at least one major investing institution has attempted a sound analysis of a new product and has opened the door to the developer and surveyor with a new scheme to sell. The managers of a new special fund will without doubt be very selective for obvious reasons and will certainly be expecting an extremely professional presentation of proposals. The main elements of such a presentation should include:

Market research findings
- end-user requirements
- competition
- demand.

Conceptual design and layout Marketing strategy
- objectives
- target
- promotional plan
- timescale

Pricing strategy
- objectives
- rents
- special deals
- competitive positioning

Construction costs and timescale
Monitoring and management

The above bears a strong similarity to the kind of presentation that an industrial company would expect when giving instructions to an agent for the disposal of a property, or a major developer planning a retail or office development. Not surprisingly, the format constitutes a basic approach of the marketer on any new product development activity, and certain elements are, of course, familiar to the surveyor and valuer.

Chapter 4. References.
[1] "The Practice of Estate Agency". Nigel Stephens. The Estates Gazette Ltd. 1980.
[2] "Property & Technology — The Needs of Modern Industry". Herring Son & Daw. 1982.
[3] "Modern Methods of Valuation". Britton, Davies and Johnson. The Estates Gazette Ltd. 1980.
[4] United Kingdom Property Report 1983. Richard Ellis.
[5] Estates Gazette Property Review 1982. January 22nd 1983.
[6] John Winkler. Pricing Strategy. "Marketing". April 14th 1983.
[7] "Buildings for Industry". Centre for Advanced Land Use Studies. College of Estate Management. 1979.
[8] "Institutions and Science Parks". John Parry. Chartered Surveyor Weekly. March 10th 1983.

CHAPTER 5
Marketing the Practice

This chapter is concerned with the marketing of the professional practice and its staff to the consumer. Why is this important? The answer is simply that the property profession cannot offer a manufactured product to a selected market where such features as durability, quality and hence future profits will ultimately depend. The marketing of professional services requires a different approach.

John Stapleton in his book *Marketing*[1], published in 1975, makes the following statement about the marketing of professional services: "It is a paradox of modern life that the very area in which marketing has been practised the longest is the one that has acquired a reputation for lack of awareness of modern marketing techniques". This may be an extreme view, but as regards the property world it is not entirely undeserved. I am conscious of the fact that young surveyors and valuers are only just beginning to receive basic training in marketing skills, but these are still limited to property disposal rather than the broader concepts of earning a living in the profession. Many established practices make little attempt to recognise that marketing applies as much to the offering of expert services and to the successful development of the practice as it does to the successful disposal of property.

Referring to the momentum of the letting of new developments the Richard Ellis report[2] says: "At these formative stages, the momentum has to be nurtured by astute marketing techniques, which are akin to the skills required to market an innovative product or service". The writer then recognises that specialist skills are required to market products or services. The *Estates Gazette* review of 1982 carries an article by the chairman of Property World about the residential market. On the subject of the house-building industry being dominated by a few giants, he states: "All of these, [giants] to survive, have drastically improved their marketing skills. . . . Most have direct sales operations with no estate agent involved." I find this rather strange in that the consumer actually probably feels that housebuilders are much more market orientated than estate agents. Barratt Homes would be a good example in support of this view. Is the truth actually that housebuilders have felt it necessary to "cut out" the agent and to build their own sales operation? If an estate agent is not a salesman then what is he?

It seems a shame to "write-off" this significant development in the estate agencies' arena. If I was a residential agent, I would be very concerned that the "giants" felt that they could do without my services. Will the chairman of Property World adopt the same attitude to the takeover by Black Horse Agencies? His only advice in the article is to say that "the estate agent will undoubtedly have to use all his skills in 1983 to convert agreed sales into completed sales and hence profit".

As I have said before, any person who offers a service for which he or she is paid a fee is a salesman. An individual or a practice that accepts this simple fact and incorporates a marketing philosophy into their business will be able to combat the housebuilders on their own terms. It is the failure of professional practices to recognise that their prime concern is to provide a service to all levels and types of consumer that is inhibiting the successful development of the profession. This is why Barratt and Wimpey have taken business away from the estate agent and it is also why the property profession in the United States is so successful. There is consolation, however, in that there are other British industries and professions still suffering from the same internal confusion as to what their real objectives are.

The problem facing a professional service industry is that at the time of commissioning, the businessman, investor or householder is not sure what he has bought. He feels the expectation that his problem may be solved and he depends upon trust. The real achievement of a successful professional service organisation is in overcoming the "credibility gap", and the true professional surveyor starts to reduce this by showing himself capable of truly understanding the real problems facing his client.

The agent demonstrates his skill by being familiar with the prospective purchaser's business and technology and not by offering services or premises which are inapplicable. With a vendor, the impression must be created that the agent knows the market, and can aim the promotional campaign of the premises or development at the right market sector. In the case of institutional clients, the practice never presents a scheme that is not well researched, well presented and fulfils the client's investment criteria.

Winning confidence is an important part of marketing professional services, and a key factor in this is image. As John

Stapleton says, "Clean and attractive premises, modern equipment, warmth and comfort, civility from staff and attention to the true interests of clients could benefit many [practices]".

Another aspect which I find disturbing is that certain commercial practices, while enjoying the benefits of a successful agency department, are not wholly committed to a commercial, let alone a marketing, philosophy. It is said that some senior partners feel that agency work is not really professional and that the status of the practice depends really upon the reputation and level of expertise of its "professional" staff. That may have been true once — many professions grew by the successful expansion of expert services with agency work being almost incidental. Consumers were in the main ignorant of these services and impressed by the views of the professional man. I do not believe this to be the case now, especially at a time when economic pressure is causing many buyers of professional services to review their requirements.

The marketing philosophy must be adopted by the whole practice in order to ensure survival in the 1980s and beyond. Every partner is committed merely by being a member of the top management group of a business enterprise. However, the task is doubly difficult for the commercial and residential agent as the RICS code of practice still views promotion of the practice itself as unethical. The Monopolies Commission, it will be remembered, also claimed that many professional groups were, in reality, restrictive practices and not acting in the public interest. An image problem was created here, rightly or wrongly.

Before proceeding further, a word about the commercial/professional conflict in the property practice. Fully appreciating how the terms have arisen and what they each mean to a surveyor, the point I wish to make is that in the eyes of the consumer, there is no difference between the commercial and the professional side of the practice. Customers who have contact with the practice expect it to be professional and demand to be treated accordingly. They are all consumers, differing only in their requirements, although they all have basic expectations of the practice, which can be summarised as follows:

(a) They each have a need that can be satisfied, at a profit.
(b) They are each prepared to pay for expert services, some with their company's money and some with their own money.
(c) They each expect, and will ultimately demand, an efficient service irrespective of the amount of money that this will cost.

(d) They can all switch from one practice to another almost at will if the service they expect is not available.
(e) They will describe the quality and cost of the service they receive to other potential customers.
(f) They are all influenced by image and approach.

5.1. Image

It is of little use pretending that the image of the commercial or residential agent is a good one. The Consumer's Association report published in *Which?* in May 1979 stated: "The most common complaints (among nearly 3,000 consumers) were that the estate agent did not work hard enough at selling the property and that he charged too much for the work he did". Whether this is a fair criticism or not, in the eyes of one in three consumers in the survey the complaint was felt to be valid. Nigel Stephens, in *The Practice of Estate Agency*[3], discusses this and the Monopolies Commission report at great length, attempting to justify such matters as fees. All this is irrelevant if, in the opinion of the consumer, a cost-effective and professional service is not being received. The consumer will look for other ways and means to satisfy his requirements, whether they be for advice or for selling property.

In the letting of commercial/industrial property there are disturbing similarities, in that many activities pursued by the residential agent are taken up by the commercial agent. This is not surprising, as often both are chartered surveyors or incorporated valuers and many practices undertake both areas of work. Differences occur in such matters as to who pays for advertising or special brochures. Fees, of course, can be extremely high and I wonder how many companies attempting to dispose of premises via commercial agents would react in the same way as the residential vendors in the *Which?* survey.

The Consumer's Association make another incredible statement in their report on estate agents, which is a clear indication of image. Referring to times when the market is booming, the report says: "In times like this don't just rely on the estate agents' mailing lists — contact them frequently, let them know you are a serious buyer". The marketing surveyor would never need reminding that a serious buyer should be cultivated. Yet I believe that the lack of enthusiasm in response to enquiries and their subsequent nurturing aptly describes the rather passive attitude of many professional property practices in both the residential and industrial/commercial fields.

Image problems occur in various, perhaps unexpected, places. Writing in the magazine *Marketing* in January 1983, George Pitcher[4] refers to the brave attempts by the New Homes Marketing Board to persuade the public to buy new houses. Picking up the point made by the NHMB chairman that every new home in 1983 will create at least two new jobs, Pitcher says: "My fear is that many of these new jobs will be in estate agents, which never seem to have any trouble making a profit". This remark may be founded upon personal experience, hearsay or nothing at all but, nevertheless, it is an indication of the kind of image agents can acquire.

On the subject of estate agents' activities on behalf of vendors, Nigel Stephens criticises those who "take instructions, prepare particulars, insert an advertisement and then just wait for things to happen". He maintains that the agent "must keep in touch" with the vendor — standard practice for any salesman in commerce or industry.

The agent's existing image, then, is not good, even accounting for any bias in the above observations. Unfortunately, property professionals often seem to share with solicitors the unenviable and ultimately fatal reputation of being unhelpful, uninterested and overpriced. Can the image be changed? I believe that it can.

5.2. The competitive edge

Let us start from the premise that everyone in the practice will fully incorporate a marketing philosophy into every aspect of service and expertise of the business; that our practice will be a consumer-orientated service machine, not an out-dated "stuffy" body; and that we will buy-in or hire the additional expertise we need or train our staff in those skills that we have recognised as being important to our enterprise. We will, of course, have researched and identified a particular market "gap" that we, as a practice, feel we can profitably fill.

Our objective is to create a good image of ourselves as professionals among the potential customers in that market. We will do this by establishing a "competitive edge", which can be described as the reason why customers will come to our practice rather than our competitors. It can take many forms, but for our business these are confined to somewhat abstract items as we are unable to offer the tangible benefits normally associated with consumer or industrial products. Nevertheless, let us examine those aspects upon which our practice could build a competitive edge. In examining each item, we should constantly ask ourselves if we can realistically and cost-effectively exploit or improve that item to give us the edge. We are seeking both new and repeat business. We remember another good maxim — "marketing is providing a product that does not come back to customers that do."

(a) Market Knowledge

A sound knowledge of the particular market that we have identified will clearly be of great advantage to us. Information will come from a number of sources and must be updated regularly. Some sources will have provided data earlier during our assessment of market viability. Figure 10 shows the typical sources of information available.

Market knowledge will help us to:
- (i) relate to potential customers;
- (ii) ensure that customer requirements are understood;
- (iii) "price" our services;
- (iv) assess current and future demand; and
- (v) focus our promotional planning

The achievement of these five items will immediately provide us with an edge over our competitors. How many professional practices can claim to have that level of market knowledge?

(b) Product Knowledge

At the same time as we build our market knowledge we gain more information on the "product". This will be either the item that we are going to market, such as industrial premises, or the service that we are going to provide — the identification of development sites, for example.

Figure 10 Sources of market knowledge

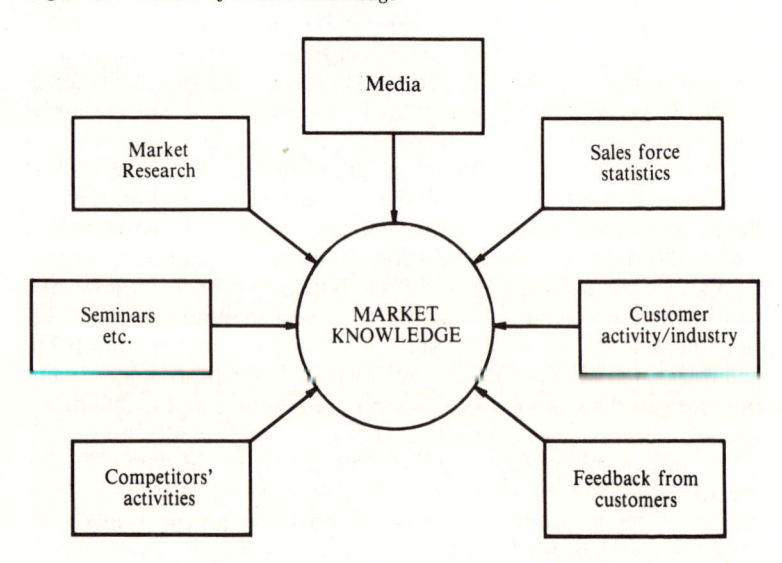

The purpose of this exercise is to establish the strengths and weaknesses of our product and to identify those features able to be turned into benefits for the customer. The detailed examination of the particular service that we are going to provide ensures that we play down its weaknesses and exploit its strengths. This can apply equally to the presentation of a potential development site to an institution, the promotional planning for disposal of premises or the offering of expert advice, ranging from valuation to project management.

This methodical procedure will add to our competitive edge by ensuring that we have the right "product" for our target market. We will build a reputation for our practice of being "on the ball" and professionally capable.

(c) Staff

A considerable edge can be gained by a realistic review of the staff in our practice and of their various roles. Our basic objective is to ensure that potential customers are treated properly. By this we mean that they, the customers, can never be wrong on any aspect. They may be misguided or difficult but must always be made to feel that they are the most important thing to our practice.

This attitude to customers starts with the telephonist or receptionist and goes through our qualified staff, trainees and surveyors, to the senior partners. At all levels we will be determined to ensure that courtesy, enthusiasm and concern are standard procedure. Any deviation from this will be subject to severe disciplinary measures. The service will apply to all levels of customer, from the old lady looking at house details for pleasure to the managing director of a company looking for an office block. Customer discrimination is both arrogant and dangerous.

American real-estate salesmen talk of 50 or so personal attributes necessary to undertake estate agency work properly. I think this is rather overdone and would advocate instead a more manageable group of essential characteristics:

    (i) Appearance
    (ii) Attitude
    (iii) Communicative ability
    (iv) Loyalty
    (v) Enthusiasm

From these five basic characteristics every other aspect springs. All staff in our practice must satisfy these five criteria irrespective of experience and qualifications.

The senior partnership in our practice also has staff responsibilities which, when undertaken seriously, will ensure that staff continue to maintain and develop these characteristics, thus giving us another competitive edge. Can all practices claim that all their staff fit these criteria? If not, what can be done?

Motivation is a critical factor. Many practices depend upon commissions, which are viewed perhaps by the staff as wage subsidies rather than incentives. Some make cars available which are often viewed as incentives when, in reality, the provision of vehicles is often a tax convenience for the partnership rather than a method of motivating staff.

In our practice we will again take a lesson from the consumer industry by assessing several incentive schemes and presenting them to the staff as a series of options. The appearance of staff could be enhanced by a clothing incentive scheme, or vehicles could be selected by the sales team on an individual basis, thus ensuring personal identity and well-being. Other schemes offer vouchers which can be saved and exchanged for luxury goods or holidays abroad, these two examples benefiting the families of staff, an area which should always be in the forefront of senior partners' minds if they want enthusiasm and loyalty.

At regular intervals throughout the year we will organise social events as part of our promotional programme. These may range from golf tournaments to river boat trips and will be primarily for the benefit of staff and their families, because we want to show our appreciation and we want the families to be involved in our business. Clients and past customers and their families will also be invited because we want to show that we are human and that we have wives and children just like them. Our objective in all this is to motivate our staff to strive harder, thus benefiting themselves and our practice. All that is required is imagination and concern.

The other important aspect of staff efficiency is training. Apart from the obvious training procedure already established for surveyors and valuers, much can be gained by introducing staff to new areas which will give them both confidence and challenge. Courses on marketing are an obvious choice for senior staff, especially those responsible for strategic management and planning functions.

For sales staff, many excellent courses are arranged by the Institute of Marketing giving an introduction to selling and the improvement of techniques. One course that runs fairly regularly covers the selling of a professional service. The institute also run courses for telephonists and receptionists, who form an integral part of the sales team structure. Other organisations such as trade associations organise sessions on new developments in technology, production techniques, etc, which I feel are especially valuable in attempting to understand what various industries will require from a surveyor or valuer by way of both premises and services.

Training, however, is not only sending staff on courses. In our practice, we shall make one of our associates or partners responsible for staff training and his or her responsibilities will be:

(i) Identifying and organising training courses, both in-house and external.
(ii) Monitoring staff development and implementing techniques.
(iii) Reporting to the partner group.
(iv) Budgeting for training.

Our competitive edge could very easily be based upon our staff and the way in which each member does his or her job.

(d) Sales

A competitive edge may be achieved by improving our sales activities (Chapter 9 will deal with the setting-up and operation of the sales office in detail). The way in which we will present our "product" to the target market will be important: first impressions do count and often only one chance is given.

The standard and availability of sales support material must ensure that potential customers have the right literature at the right time. In my experience many practices produce literature for premises that they have been instructed to sell but few for promoting other services of the firm. Supporting material should also be made available covering those aspects important to the customers in our target market. For example, prospective purchasers of retail premises would value written information on shopping patterns, public transport, suppliers, etc.

Every member of our practice also have a responsibility for client and customer relations, presenting yet another area for the establishment of a competitive edge, as many firms do not pay enough attention to this function. Customer relations is more than courtesy and enthusiasm, it also requires tenacity, especially in situations where decisions may take months to be made. Record-keeping and progress-chasing are normal functions for sales staff where a relationship needs to be nurtured to fruition, even if a sale does not accrue as a result. In our practice we should be conscious of the fact that today's vendor may be tomorrow's purchaser and that although the retail group did not like the premises we offered this month they may be very interested in what we offer next month.

Potential customers in our target market who express a definite intention to purchase are given top priority. The salesman in our team allocated to that enquirer will keep close contact and report progress regularly to his superior. He will be responsible for developing the relationship and using his sales training to its fullest extent to monitor progress and to diagnose changes in the customer's requirements and preceptions. An enquiry will never be considered to be "dead" by our practice, even when the requirements of the customer may have been satisfied on this occasion, perhaps somewhere else. We are also seeking repeat business.

Sales staff and all those concerned with customer and client relations must be involved in hosting or entertaining at some stage. This is a common and accepted courtesy in the commercial world, requiring only a basic set of guidelines for staff to follow and an appreciation by the partners of the value of such activities to successful business.

(e) Special services

In the examination of those aspects of our business that we feel would form the basis for a competitive edge, we have so far considered features that exist in one form or another in most of our competitors' operations. We have contemplated expansion of those features to make us more successful and have critically assessed our ability to build and maintain a competitive advantage. Our competitors, of course, could be undertaking a similar exercise capable of eclipsing our own efforts.

What else then could we do to gain new business? The emphasis must be on cost-effectiveness, as any special services that we provide must be profitable in their own right or capable of producing profit via ancillary services — a kind of "loss-leader" approach.

Let us assume that we have identified a consumer need in the industrial and commercial field for certain services not currently provided by the surveyor's profession but of considerable importance to a potential buyer of property. The setting-up and operation of special services should present no problem to us, as we already offer expertise in the basic skills such as valuation, rating, structural surveys, etc, but what about other services? We must not feel inhibited by our profession as long as we do not stray into areas which are clearly outside the capabilities of our staff, in which case we either steer clear or buy in the necessary expertise.

For the industrial and consumer buyer we could consider providing the following services:

(i) Funding. In drawing together a funding package for a potential buyer, our sources would include merchant banks, ICFC, government grants, etc, as well as resources within the company itself. Certain of our competitors already do something along these lines, but we will do it better by adopting the stance of a "funding

manager", ensuring that only the most applicable and advantageous sources are used and by arranging a follow-through to fruition. We will not simply provide our customer with a list of addresses and telephone numbers.

(ii) Staff recruitment. Virtually every purchaser of industrial or commercial property will be recruiting staff of some kind. But staff recruitment and wage levels can be difficult for companies who move to new locations. To our knowledge, our competitors are not providing a service in this area, other than supplying the address of the local job centre. We could therefore set up an advisory unit to assist with recruitment.

(iii) Utility services. The arranging of gas, electricity, water and telecommunications services can be a time-consuming and often frustrating activity for companies acquiring new premises. Could we take this headache away by providing a "services" service? Again we find our competitors simply listing the addresses of utilities, suggesting that companies make their own arrangements.

(iv) Suppliers. Modern industries are users of a whole range of components with buyers constantly searching for local suppliers of the right calibre, not just because of cost reductions resulting from ease of distribution but also because most companies do not carry large stocks any more and a supplier "down the road" can respond to a telephone request more quickly than a supplier 100 miles away. Local servicing and support services are also important to major companies.

As far as we can ascertain, the provision of information on suppliers has never really been considered to be within the sphere of activity of the property practice. Yet would this not be a good platform for our sales thrust? As soon as we have identified a possible purchaser for premises that we are promoting we could put together a document giving details of relevant suppliers and their products, capacity etc.

(v) Removals. Like the arranging of services, moving plant, equipment, furniture and fittings from one place to another can be a time-consuming affair for management. As the property agents, could we not arrange all this for a prospective purchaser? Our service could include special skills such as the removal and setting-up of major computer installations.

The final question with regard to the provision of special services is, who pays? It could be the purchaser himself who, having agreed to buy, then commissions us to help with staff recruitment for example, or, alternatively, a client may be persuaded to pay for research into components suppliers to service a company in the premises that we are attempting to let. On his instructions, we would have already focused our promotion on a particular sector. This would apply equally to industrial or commercial premises — they all need suppliers. Thirdly, we might agree as a policy to provide a service for nothing, on the basis that this clear competitive advantage would make us more successful at premises disposal and we would therefore attract more instructions. If this latter decision is taken then we must plan carefully and allocate the necessary resources.

(f) Charges

Recent legislation and the more liberal attitude of the RICS and ISVA leave the question of charges wide open for the development of a competitive edge. As a professional practice we must initially decide what our objectives are in terms of earning revenue. We can either continue with the traditional scales of charges, thus risking criticism and possibly an uncertain future, or we decide to reduce charges and go for volume business in order to increase income.

If we adopt the latter policy, then we must examine each component of our revenue-earning portfolio with a view to developing a competitive pricing strategy. We will consider:

(i) Fees for property disposal
(ii) Retainers
(iii) Commissions
(iv) Fees for special services

Changes to any of these four must be acceptable in the market place, as there is a pricing point at which buyers will not trust the "product". In addition we must make sure that our new arrangement will bring in the necessary volume of business and that the projected income will cover the costs of its provision as well as contribute to profit.

5.3. Image building

Earlier in this chapter I discussed image in connection with the somewhat biased views of certain groups or individuals. Having accepted that image is important to the property practice, let us examine ways and means in which image can be improved or changed.

I have already covered those aspects of image-building that are projected by the establishment of a competitive edge through the professionalism of the staff, but there are other activities which should be regarded as complimentary to the staff function.

(i) Corporate identity

The adoption of a house style or colours that will present the desired image is important. Most agents depend upon site boards to advertise properties but in my view pay insufficient attention to the image that this creates.

Having established a corporate style, the perception in the eyes of the customers of security and reliability can be portrayed by using the design on all visible material. This also has the effect of building a kind of "brand loyalty", whereby the logo or style of a particular firm becomes associated with its good attributes.

(ii) Advertising the practice

Promoting the practice by advertising is still considered to be unethical by the property institutions. Nigel Stephens claims that if agents were allowed to advertise themselves in a free-for-all situation then the effectiveness of the advertising would somehow diminish, but this is not the case in the consumer industry, where competing companies often advertise similar products simultaneously.

The purpose of advertising is simply to persuade groups of consumers to buy the products of company "A" as opposed to those of company "B", and elements such as product features, durability or price, form the basis for encouraging consumers to switch from one brand to another. I see no reason why the same principles should not apply to commercial or residential agents, so that marketing-orientated practices with innovation and flair use advertising as a means of communicating their skills and services to potential customers. In the United States, many professional institutions once fought shy of corporate or image advertising, but a limited form is now generally acceptable and does not appear to have affected the professional standing of the practices involved.

(iii) Press relations

The use of what is termed press relations techniques is now well established as a means of free advertising, and is another form of communicating with potential customers. I have covered the uses and types of techniques in Chapter 8, so it is necessary here only to establish that the same techniques can be used to promote the practice as well as to promote a property or development scheme. The difference is really a matter of content and style. For example, articles for the property press would be prepared with the intention of impressing readers, who themselves are property people, that the writer (and hence his practice) is both professional and authoritative. A press release in a local business paper, however, may cover the attributes of a development scheme — the intention, of course, being to attract potential buyers.

(iv) Sponsorship

Until recently the domain of consumer industries, sponsorship of various events is now common practice for banks and insurance companies. The purpose is to portray an image of public involvement and support, thus impressing potential customers, and to use the events to invite clients and associates for a day out. Many sports now receive wide television coverage, attracting sponsors who believe that free advertising in the mass media constitutes value for money.

There may be a place for quality sponsorship for the professional practice if selected carefully. Large sums of money can be involved and the practice must determine in advance what benefits will accrue from the sponsorship. Local cultural events seem to appeal as being most productive, although there is always the risk of public criticism.

(v) Exhibitions

Altogether a more acceptable form of promoting the practice than sponsorship, exhibitions are rarely exploited by property practices. Chapter 8 explains how to use exhibitions to promote premises, but they can also be very effective in promoting the practice. They should not be viewed purely as a sales pitch for property developments. The image of the practice, with its expert and special services, as well as the offices and staff can be imaginatively promoted via exhibitions at a reasonable cost.

(vi) Personal recommendations

This aspect of image-building is the back-stop for many professional practices and yet how badly it is exploited. Personal recommendation is important in developing an image of professionalism and reliability and it seems to be as valuable to the industrial and commercial practice as it is to the residential.

Recommendations must initially depend upon the way in which customers are dealt with by staff. Enthusiasm and professionalism will nurture this first impression and a successful outcome will ensure that a good recommendation is passed on. One must accept, however, that recommendations are emotive and often based upon personal experience. It is essential that every person in the practice is aware of his or her role in ensuring that the personal recommendation is an integral part of the image-building process.

Europe's largest estate agency, Mann & Co, obviously appreciate the value of good image-building. An article in *Marketing*[5] reported that they have decided to use local radio in the Reading area as an alternative to traditional press advertising. What is interesting is that they examined their source of sales and found that most came through their High Street offices. As Colin Stovold, Mann's area director, said, "We register at least 500 new customers in the South East every day, so we're never short of buyers. What we're concerned with, therefore, is our public image". Funnily enough in the same article, the writer refers to the "new threat from Lloyds Bank Black Horse chain of estate agents". Pointing out the likely outcome if more clearing banks follow suit, he continues: "existing agents will need to take a long hard look at the way they present themselves".

5.4. Attacking the market

By way of a summation, it is necessary to refer to a couple of items from previous chapters which have implications for the way in which the practice markets itself. At this stage, I am not outlining the promotional techniques; these are contained in Chapter 8.

In planning out the way in which the practice itself is marketed, objectives will have been established, the competition assessed and the particular area of demand estimated. It is unlikely that the objectives will be achieved by the use of a "passive" approach to marketing. Passive in this sense means a responsive attitude to customers — the kind of thing that Nigel Stephens meant in referring to those agents who advertise property and then just "wait for things to happen". Passive sales staff regard telephones merely as equipment for incoming calls. They respond only to action by a customer and never follow up enquiries: the customer is left instead to pursue his own requirements.

An "aggressive" policy, however, does not automatically mean the employment of "hard-sell" methods. Many commercial agents seem afraid of aggressive techniques, but I suspect that this is based on an instinctive abhorrence of the used-car-salesman image that seems to surround every successful sales practitioner. Neither do aggressive techniques imply a door-knocking campaign to drum up new business: in any event, this is still against the code of practice of both the RICS and the ISVA and may be unacceptable to the British public at large.

In the industrial and commercial property fields, mailshots to companies and retail groups are an established, and potentially ineffective, method of reaching an unfocused market. Mailshots are strictly a passive activity, but targeted mailshots with personal follow-up by telephone or visit are "aggressive".

The introduction and development of aggressive techniques have their foundations in the very core of the practice, and Chapter 9 covers the operation of a sales office based upon the assumption that an aggressive policy has been adopted and that the right staff have been recruited.

Finally, it is worth considering how the role of a practice may change in response to economic and social pressures, for an appreciation of the implications of such changes will influence the decisions taken in connection with the marketing of the practice. In times of recession, invariably allied with shortages and inflation and conveniently referred to by American economists as "stagflation", most companies adopt one of three courses of counteraction.

(i) Demarketing

This involves cutting back on new product development, market research and product quality; prices go up and service goes down. There is an immediate short-term increase in profits but customer loyalty suffers irreparably and long-term objectives become meaningless.

(ii) "Do-nothing" approach

Such an approach is based on a false expectation that the recession is only temporary and that eventually things will return to normal. While customer goodwill is maintained, this attitude is unrealistic and not in the company's long-term interest.

(iii) Strategic remarketing

A phrase coined by Philip Kotler, this method advocates a top management re-think of the company's policies on customer mix, product mix and marketing mix. For the property practice this could mean a re-evaluation of its customer/client portfolio, the expert services offered by the practice and its promotional activities both of services and of premises.

The main effects of this reassessment can be interpreted into specific tasks. Sales staff will find that their roles will change but without becoming less important to the practice. On the contrary, the flexible and aggressive salesman who can change roles to suit conditions is a tremendous asset when times are tough. Has the basic selling technique in the chartered surveyor's practice altered in response to "stagflation"?

Changes in established consumer practices such as market research and new product development seem rather inappropriate for the property profession as so little is currently undertaken. Market research and segmentation become very important during recession for the speculative developer of industrial and commercial property, because the market becomes smaller, selective, and more difficult to cultivate. For the surveyor the additional need to improve and exploit services during recession may be critical to economic survival.

Chapter 5. References

[1] "Marketing". John Stapleton. Hodder & Stoughton Paperbacks 1979.
[2] United Kingdom Property Report 1983. Richard Ellis.
[3] "The Practice of Estate Agency". Nigel Stephens. The Estates Gazette Ltd. 1980.
[4] Marketer's Diary. George Pitcher. "Marketing". January 13th 1983.
[5] "Marketing". January 6th 1983.

1. Industrial units, New Jersey

2. Princeton Corporate Centre, New Jersey

3. *Forbury Industrial Park, Reading*

4. *Industrial Units, Gloucester*

5. *Office Units, Santa Clara*

6. *Industrial Units, San José*

7. Forbury Industrial Park, Reading

8. Innsworth Technology Park, Gloucester

9. Industrial Units, San José

10. Industrial/Office block. San José

11. *Industrial Units, Reading*

12. *The Genesis Project, Warrington*

A development by Starwars Ltd

CANAL SCIENCE PARK

A Unique Opportunity

NEW FREEHOLD INDUSTRIAL PREMISES

Suitable for Hi-Tech industry or Warehousing (or anything)

* Strategically located
* Impressive reception area
* Units available from 500-50,000 sq. ft.
* Prestiguous car park
* Fully landscaped
* High quality

The site has excellent communications with the M87 motorway and other major road links which provide excellent access to all major U.K. markets. Train to Central London is $5\frac{1}{2}$ hours by regular Inter-city service, and the International Airport provides regular scheduled services to Europe and the U.K.

Please contact the agents for further information.

House Marketing & Co.

20 Nonsuch Street
Anytown
Landshire KX1 4EN

13. *"Persuasive advertising"*

A VERY SPECIAL PACKAGE

Hoechst House
Hounslow

14. *The package approach*

15. The personal approach

WOODLANDS WORKSHOP CENTRE

COED CAE LANE, PONTYCLUN, MID GLAMORGAN

A NEW CONCEPT IN THE PROVISION OF INDUSTRIAL SPACE

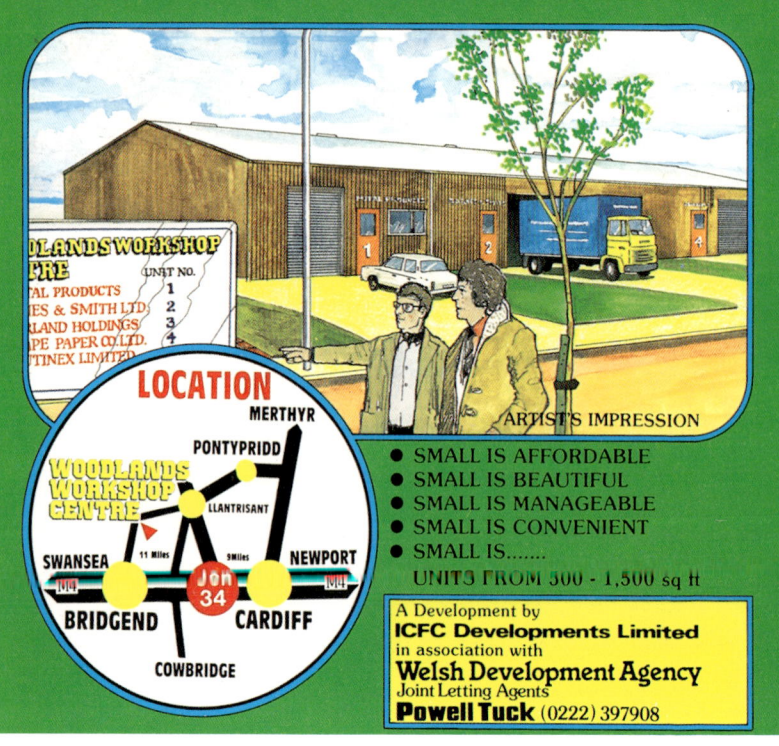

ARTIST'S IMPRESSION

- SMALL IS AFFORDABLE
- SMALL IS BEAUTIFUL
- SMALL IS MANAGEABLE
- SMALL IS CONVENIENT
- SMALL IS.......

UNITS FROM 300 - 1,500 sq ft

A Development by
ICFC Developments Limited
in association with
Welsh Development Agency
Joint Letting Agents
Powell Tuck (0222) 397908

16. *Too many clichés?*

Freehold for Sale or to Let

Prestige Headquarters Premises

on the instructions of

GRUNDIG International Limited

40/42 Newlands Park, Sydenham SE 26

The property enjoys a double frontage to Studland Road and Newlands Park, close to Sydenham Hill shopping centre, and within close proximity to Crystal Palace and Croydon. Sydenham and Penge East southern region railway stations are both within easy reach and numerous bus routes serve the area.

17. *Difficult to read?*

WDA
Welsh Development Agency

INTRODUCING **TECHBASE**

AN EXTENSIVELY RESEARCHED
GROWTH-INDUSTRY DEVELOPMENT
DESIGNED BY
POTENTIAL USERS

18. *Emphasis on market research*

On Behalf of Chicopee Limited.

SOUTH WALES
BLACKWOOD GWENT

Put down roots and grow…

19. *Sounds familiar*

Baglan
Industrial Park
WDA

A prestige development

20. Impact photography

MASONS HILL, BROMLEY
LINDEN HOUSE & MAPLE HOUSE
To let as a whole or individually

A unique campus-style office development by Barratt Properties

Barratt

21. *Campus-style artists' impression*

22. *Close encounters*

GREATER LONDON & ESSEX NEWSPAPERS LTD., WEDNESDAY, JUNE 29, 1983

GREATER LONDON AND ESSEX 1983
Business News

Lettings at Gallows Corner

Morrison Developments have now completed an industrial and warehouse development known as the Stafford Estate.

The estate at Gallows Corner, Romford, benefits from an excellent location, being less than half a mile from Gallows Corner flyover and within three miles of the recently opened M25 intersections with the A127 and the A12.

Joint agents Richard Ellis and Henry Berney report a good level of interest with the first letting imminent and a further two units firmly under offer.

Negotiations are in progress for a number of the other units at rentals in the region of £3 to £3.50 per sq. ft.

Cowdray CENTRE
Colchester
New Development

TO LET

Features:
- Situated on the inner ring-road
- Close to BR Station and town centre
- Self-contained
- All mains services
- Ample car parking
- Short lets can be arranged
- Available Now
- First class access to A12, East Coast Ports and M25.

Industrial/Warehouse
UNITS FROM
3,290 sq.ft. - 23,000 sq.ft.

SELF CONTAINED UNITS
18,620 sq.ft. including
4,200 sq.ft. OFFICES

Cowdray CENTRE COLCHESTER

Fenn Wright — 146 High Street, Colchester, Essex CO1 1PW. Telephone (0206) 46161

Richard Ellis — Chartered Surveyors. 6-10 Bruton Street, London W1X 8DU. Telephone 01-408 0921

Your best move NOW...

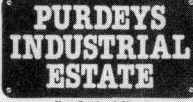

PURDEYS INDUSTRIAL ESTATE
Near Southend Airport

...and for the future!

Excellent links with London and the Continent

* Low maintenance costs
* Room for future expansion
* Capital Equipment & Vehicle Leasing facilities at reduced rates for new tenants
* Fixed Term service charges
* Custom built or Standard premises
* Full 'Package Deal' if required
* A MAJOR DEVELOPMENT BY
* Lease redemption schemes

Rochehall
LTD.
2 Purdeys Way, Rochford
Essex, SS4 1NE
Tel: (0702) 546534

Big store 'doubles up' at Purdeys

Purdeys Industrial Estate, Rochford, Essex is near Southend Airport on the outskirts of Southend. Twenty acres have so far been developed, leaving 32 acres available for the future.

Whenever the developers, Rochehall Limited, build new or larger units, many of these are taken up by existing tenants requiring larger or additional premises. This is made easier by the policy of the developers in taking back unwanted, unexpired leases from lessees who wish to expand into larger premises on the estate.

As well as manufacturing and service industries, vital to the area's economic growth, the Estate has become established as an out-of-town Retail area, with M.F.I., Harris Queensway and Texas Homecare all trading very satisfactorily. The M.F.I. unit is unique in that it was their very first purpose-built store and is featured in their television advertisements. Trading has been so good that M.F.I. have recently acquired a further unit, doubling their covering on this Site.

The potential of this Estate was first recognised by Mr. Claud Curtis, a Director of a local Building Company, in 1965. The land was then known as Purdeys Farm, but had been used as a commercial tip for about forty years. At that time Mr. Curtis's Company, The Hose Construction Co. Ltd., was pioneering the building of small factory units, when most Developers were only interested in large, single-occupation premises.

"But", argued Mr. Curtis, "Four or five businesses occupying the same area must have better potential for employment and expansion in this part of the country which is rich with diverse skills and an enthusiastic workforce". It is, in fact, no accident that this is considered to be one of the most affluent areas of the U.K.; it has an excellent record of low industrial discord.

A regular bus service operates from centres of Southend; there are the usual postal services, and the National Westminster Bank has an established sub-branch on the Estate. Other reasons for its success are its attractive and spacious layout, creating a pleasant working environment and its well built, quality buildings, resulting in low cost maintenance. Its location is ideal, being adjacent to Southend Airport and near the A127 Southend Arterial Road; it is easily accessible

---

Dagenham	TO LET
New Factories/Warehouses	
10,000 to 20,000 sq. ft.	
Competitive Terms.	
Joint Agents: Fuller Peiser.	

Hockley	TO LET / FOR SALE
Factory/Warehouse & Offices	
20,000 to 46,000 sq. ft.	
Modern single storey premises with good loading facilities. Fully Fitted.	

Woodford	TO LET
New Factory & Warehouse units	
4,855 to 57,000 sq. ft.	
Adjacent to M11. High Specification.	

West Thurrock	FOR SALE
Distribution & Transport Depot Near to M25	
40,250 sq. ft.	
of offices, warehouse & workshop on 4.5 acres.	
Joint Agents: C. L. Porter & Co.	

Romford	FOR SALE
Factory & Office Premises	
17,250 sq. ft. & 33,000 sq. ft.	
Good Communications	

Dagenham	TO LET
New self contained Factory/Warehouse unit	
5,500 sq. ft.	
Fully Fitted	
Joint Agents: Fuller Peiser	

King & Co
1 Snow Hill, London EC1A 2DL
01-236 3000

24. *Aiming at the family*

Johnson Kelly

Surveyors, Estate Agents & Auctioneers

'THE OLD TOWN HALL, BLACKBURN'

North West Property Guide

25. Is this for sale?

Winter 1982-83

JLW
COMMERCIAL PROPERTY
TO LET
OR
FOR SALE

Jones Lang Wootton
Chartered Surveyors · International Real Estate Consultants

West End Office   City Office
01-493 6040   **01-638 6040**

26. *Clear, positive style*

The REALTORS HOME GUIDE

REALTOR®

ISSUE 37 — SEPTEMBER, 1983

FREE

MODESTO EDITION

SPECIAL FINANCING AVAILABLE
JUST LOOK FOR THE HAPPY FACE

27. *Happy approach*

ISSUE No. 8   **DECEMBER, 1982/JANUARY, 1983**   **30p**

Estate

A MONTHLY GUIDE TO PROPERTIES IN SOUTH WALES

See page 17 for further details.

THE QUALITY HOMES MAGAZINE FOR WALES

WIN A VALUABLE ANTIQUE
(See inside for details)

28. Prestigious — with competitions!

29. Maximum information . . . .

30. Minimum information

31. Offices to lease, San José

32. Office Park, San José

33. *Wooden supports* . . . .

34. *No supports*

35. *Greentree Campus, New Jersey*

36. *Clear message at New Jersey*

37. *Impact photography*

Week by Week
Central Square

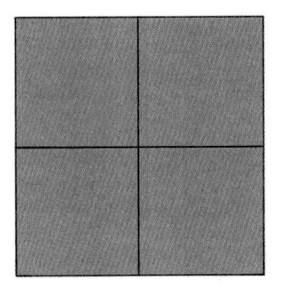

is Growing

38. Simple but effective

A development by James Longley Properties Limited
and Audley House Investments Limited

Back a Winner at Epsom!

CHARLES STUART HOUSE
Church Street, Epsom

- 11,515 square feet net (1,070sq.m.) of new office accommodation on three floors.
- Elegant appearance and very high quality construction.
- Interior office layout of precision and efficiency.
- Private courtyard with 29 parking spaces.

FURTHER DETAILS AVAILABLE FROM THE JOINT AGENTS:

Mason Philips
53 Grosvenor Street, London W1X 9FH.
01-499 9793.

Bridgers Commercial
70 High Street, Epsom, Surrey KT19 8BD.
03727-41777.

39. *Good use of location name*

40. "High-tech" image?

41. Clever use of words

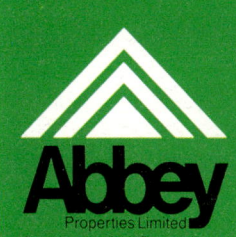

42. Interesting design

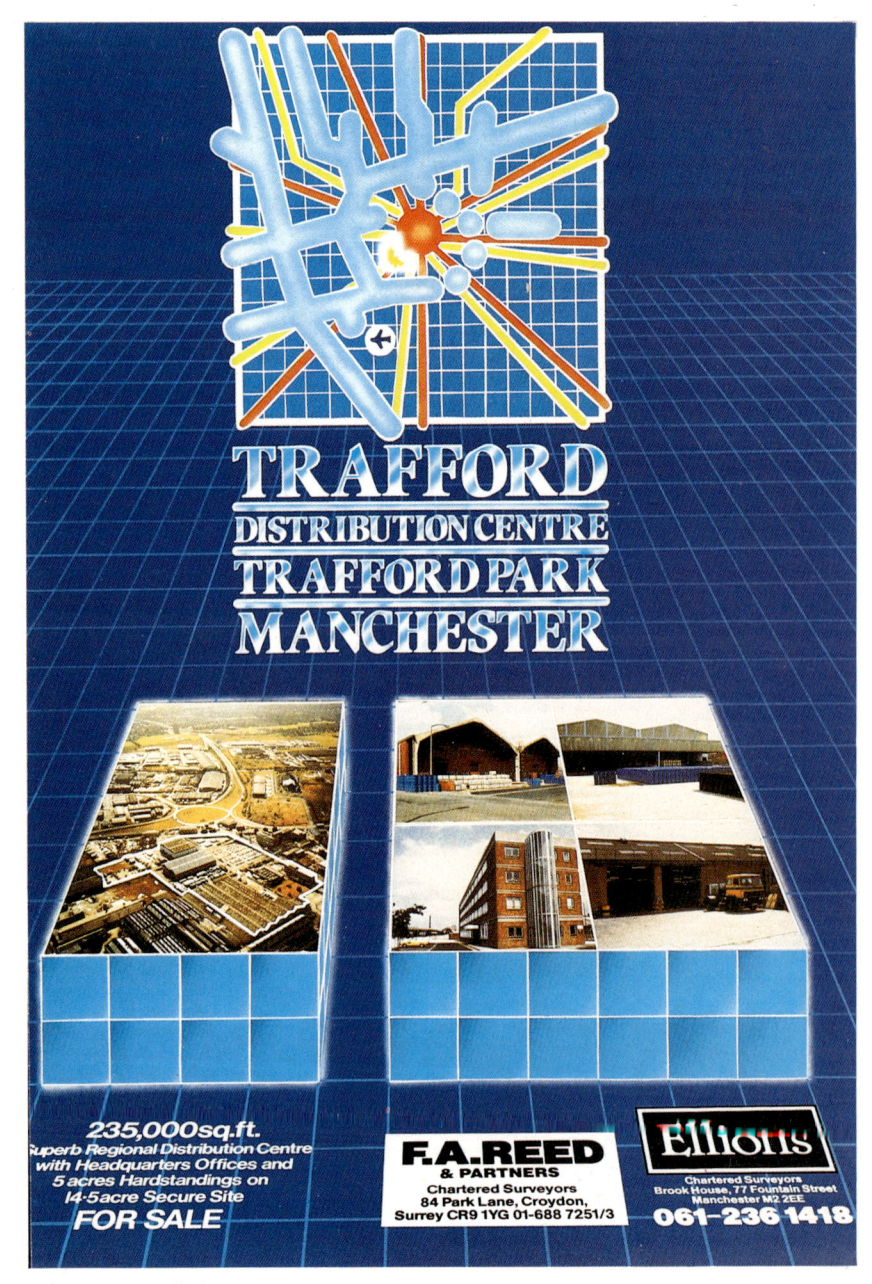

CHAPTER 6
Market Research

Market research provides the means by which consumer requirements are identified and the resulting market opportunities anticipated. It entails seeking market "gaps" and providing the information by which product needs, price and the most effective approach to the market are assessed. Market research will also establish the effectiveness of advertising and the reputation of companies in a given market place.

Research techniques all have one basic common objective — to obtain information, which may come from people, companies or governments. This objective makes market research the main component of a marketing information system comprising a number of methods designed to provide data for the marketer and his company.

Modern market research was conceived by advertising agencies who wanted to supply their clients with information to illustrate the effectiveness of advertising campaigns or to identify groups of consumers as a pre-requisite to the design of an advertising campaign. In 1979 some £80m was spent in the United Kingdom on market research — about 7p for every £100 spent by consumers. It has an essential role in all business undertakings and across all products and while the methodology may vary, from a food company researching yoghurt flavours to a weapons manufacturer ascertaining the needs of foreign governments, there are no exceptions.

Because research is such a major component of a marketing information system, it will be covered in some detail in this chapter. Before discussing uses and techniques, however, it is necessary to consider the structure of the all-important information system itself.

Systems will vary from company to company depending upon the nature of their business. Basically, the marketing information system stands between the market environment and the marketer in the company. It constitutes the structure by which all relevant intelligence data, including market research, is channelled through to the marketer and by which decisions are fed back. Intelligence relating to the buying/selling operations of the company, activities of competitors, research projects for new brands and data from facilities such as forecast-demand models are all part of the information flow that constitutes a marketing information system. The marketer has to assimilate and digest this information before he can make recommendations to top management or determine the thrust of the promotional strategy.

The need for a marketing information system becomes stronger than ever during depressed times, simply because the marketer, or his company, cannot afford to be ill-informed. Today's markets tend to be smaller and more fragmented, with fierce competition. Mistakes are expensive and misreading the market or depending upon too little information or on intuition is a dangerous and unnecessary game.

Philip Kotler[1] gives three further reasons for an efficient information system:

(a) The shift from local to international marketing, making market areas more remote from marketing executives.
(b) The transition from buyer needs to buyer wants as a direct result of increased affluency.
(c) The move from price to non-price competition where other factors relevant to quality, service and image are becoming important in certain markets.

Many firms in this country still do not have marketing information systems, or, indeed, market research departments but depend instead upon historical statistics and opinions and the occasional survey, where money is available that could not be spent upon some other requirement considered to be more important.

Market research is still considered by many as applicable to soap powder or cigarettes rather than to their own particular products. There is still the mistaken belief that the inventor of a product has, by definition, a detailed knowledge of the perceived markets for that product. His knowledge rarely extends to the price that the market will bear, the size of the market, his potential share, competition, and how to identify and approach the market. Nevertheless, numerous companies have been spectacularly successful with particular products while freely admitting that they have undertaken little or no research and see no necessity for a marketing information system in their operation. Such success stories are often without real foundation. Sinclair computers have achieved market leadership not by luck but by targeting a sector of the computer market (the home enthusiast) and pricing basic models cheaper than competitors. Sinclair knew that the home hobbyist would initially buy on price and appearance rather than technical features. Market research was certainly involved in this approach.

In the property world, many successes have been achieved without research or sound market information. There has been in the past a heavy dependence upon what a surveyor colleague of mine calls "General Understanding of the Trade" or "gut". In boom times, it seems possible to run a successful property agency with a minimum of marketing intelligence. It can also be very profitable to develop office and shopping facilities in city centres: these will let eventually. When times are bad, however, lack of good market information inhibits the agent in his letting role and much property lies empty where prospects for rent, let alone rental growth, seem very bleak.

Given that there are difficulties created by the long life of premises and that agents are currently faced with having to dispose of a large stock of redundant premises, is there a role for market research in the property profession?

In considering these questions, it is necessary to understand that any potential value of market research applies to three separate, yet interdependent, activities of the marketing surveyor or valuer:

(1) The setting-up and promotion of the practice and its expert services.
(2) Advising clients on the viability, design mix and marketing of development projects.
(3) Procedures adopted following instructions for the disposal of existing premises.

It is inevitable that an examination of the current use or non-use of research in the property profession will find evidence related mainly to new development schemes, for it is in this area that most practitioners feel that some kind of demand assessment or market knowledge would be most valuable. I do not disagree with this but I know that much more can be achieved.

Market research can be used to identify those elements important to the planning of a new branch office, for example, while the promotion of second-hand premises would also benefit from some imaginative research into potential markets. A number of applications of the techniques are possible, given the right attitude and a willingness by the surveyor to work in areas outside the scope of his formal training. He has much to gain by taking the lead in the application of market research in the property profession.

6.1. Property development

David Cadman and Leslie Austin-Crowe in their book *Property Development*[2] are quite specific about market research. At the beginning of Chapter 2 they say: "No development should be undertaken without a proper analysis of the market for which the buildings are constructed". Right in line with the philosophy of marketing and a clear recognition that the "consumer" is pretty important and necessitates some examination. They continue: "This may seem so obvious that it is hardly worth stating, but historically too little effort and expenditure has been spent on such analysis and too many projects have been undertaken entirely on 'hunches' [General Understanding of the Trade again] or on the basis that someone else has carried out a similar project successfully elsewhere".

This last sentence is very significant. The recent spate of "science parks" in this country (nearly 60 are at present either built or planned) is an excellent example of what the authors mean. Science parks are not being developed with the aid of market research; it is assumed instead that there are sufficient companies needing this kind of floorspace or that each developer will take some other competitor's share of the market. Both assumptions are without proper foundation, although I accept that a level of surplus of suitable speculative property is desirable and that efforts are being made by government institutions to expand the market by the encouragement of new start-up businesses.

Referring to the traditional development team, David Cadman and Leslie Austin-Crowe recommend that the new approach should be to include a land economist, an architect/planner, a valuer and in some cases a sociologist. They have assumed that the marketing input would be provided by the "estate agent". United States developers go further, however, and include a "marketing specialist" in the development team. Under the heading "Development Strategy" the 1980 edition of the *US Industrial Development Handbook*[3] says: "It is important to remember that determining feasibility of an industrial development requires the skill of many disciplines". So would the "marketing specialist" be the surveyor? In the United States it would seem to be so, for an example is given with a list of consultants involved in the undertaking of a development scheme in Colorado:

Planning and landscape architects
Civil engineers
Water and sewer engineers
Transportation consultants
Architects
Graphic design/marketing communications
Soil engineers
Marketing agents.

Note that "marketing communications", ie image development, brochure design etc, is seen as a separate activity to that of the letting agent. How unlike a development team in this country, where "marketing communications" would not be mentioned at all in a development project. Neither would the agent's name always appear.

How is marketing research viewed by authors on both sides of the Atlantic in connection with property development? The United Kingdom authors clearly consider that "market research is carried out to establish the nature of the property market at a particular time". They emphasise its importance to developers where market conditions are uncertain or where little existing evidence is available in specialised markets (such as high-technology?). Several specific items are then listed as constituting the research programme.

(i) General factors Local characteristics, socio/economic factors, services, transport facilities, labour.

(ii) Specific factors
  (a) *Housing* — Views of local agents, building societies, attitudes and preferences of local householders.
  (b) *Industrial* — Employment, transport, raw materials, end-user requirements.
  (c) *Shops* — Catchment area characteristics, other shops and shopping centres, end-user requirements.
  (d) *Offices* — Transport, labour supply, proximity of shopping facilities, end-user requirements.

(iii) The local authority — Detailed property inventory, trends, expert opinion, local authority objectives.

I would not disagree with the immense value of these three research areas, but I am not convinced that all property developers and their agents adopt anything like such a professional approach to their proposals. Despite the depth of research advocated by the authors, I would add a further four items that are essential to the formulation of the marketing mix prior to scheme design:

(iv) Price — An assessment of the price that the market will pay for the proposed development. This will dictate construction costs.

(v) Demand — An estimate of current and future demand, if any, as discussed in Chapter 4.

(vi) Competition — An assessment of competitor's activities with their strengths and weaknesses.

(vii) Approach — A review of the most effective channels of persuasion for the approach to the target market.

In the United States, the *Industrial Development Handbook* recommends a totally integrated approach to market research as part of the development appraisal. This entails the full scope of investigative activity being undertaken simultaneously after a potential site has been identified. The exercise would be repeated a number of times as different sites in different locations are evaluated under varying market conditions.

The main difference between the two approaches is that the Americans approach the market viability of the scheme tactically, using the appropriate specialists. They also include demand estimation and an assessment of competitor strengths in the research. The handbook recommends the following research programme:

(i) *Analysis of the competition* — Prices currently charged, take-up, land costs, after-sales service, funding arrangements, lease deals, etc.
(ii) *Economic base study* — Employment analysis and projections, impact of large local employers, relationships between local and national economic patterns.
(iii) *Transport and distribution* — Costs and availability by mode. Five-year forecast.
(iv) *Services* — Costs and availability. Five-year forecast
(v) *Local commerce and government* — Planning regulations, activities of development agencies, banks, etc.

The handbook carries a warning, however, that is worthy of repetition: "Market projections based on historical facts will not reflect the unique ability of a developer to identify a way to attract a group of related economic activities". I would never deny that instinct, flair and "gut" feel are not important. What I am saying is that such skills are no longer sufficient on their own.

Reference to market research appears at fairly regular intervals in the property industry, seeming to suggest that it is very much in the minds of established practitioners, especially those involved in future developments. Nigel Stephens[4] makes reference to the need for the effective commercial agent to be "aware of any changes, for example, in the retail shopping pattern, or in the requirements of the average industrialist or office user". He also, quite rightly, advocates that the agent must keep up to date with changes in the transport infrastructure and monitor the views and policies of the investing institutions. Clearly, he is making a case for a marketing information system, since several sources of intelligence are involved.

Failure to anticipate a recession in the house market or a significant change in investment yields is seen by Nigel Stephens as having serious consequences for an agent. The only sure way to foresee changes is to use market research.

Several references to market research were contained in the January 22 1983 issue of *Estates Gazette*. Derek Penfold, on the subject of high-technology industries, mentioned the slowness of property practitioners "to appreciate the special needs of this type of occupier". The profession had failed to anticipate a consumer requirement. "Carefully guided and researched property investment" is advocated by Paul Orchard-Lisle in referring to investment criteria. He recognises the need for research in the recommendation of investments to institutions.

Two contrasting high-tech projects currently appear to be benefiting from a level of research input. The first is at Aztec West in Bristol, where Guy Morton-Smith of Richard Ellis claims they are marketing "a modern development geared to a rapidly changing market where quality, mixed-use, flexibility, design, amenity and space are key words". One could, however, maintain that these attributes have always been key words in industrial development. The second scheme is the Cambridge Science Park, of which J V Tweddle of Bidwells says: "Companies regard it as crucial that the buildings are physically attractive, the surroundings and general ambience are pleasant, ample car parking is provided and, very importantly, each unit has its own front door and therefore its own identity".

Both the agents' statements are probably true but in my view lack credibility and therefore acceptance in the market place. Market research may have shown that if "flexibility" means high headroom then high-technology companies are less interested and that "general ambience" is desirable as long as tenants do not have to pay for landscaping maintenance. "Design" is all very well, but what about site-security, telecommunications requirements and the needs of electronics companies who use compressed-air?

Stephen Greenbury, of Newman Levinson & Partners, is an architect with an interest in high-technology buildings and science parks generally, and in the same issue of *Estates Gazette* he claims that "the high-tech tenant who takes a standard speculative unit is invariably infuriated by the inadequacies of the buildings available in the UK". This would seem to conflict with the statements made by Morton-Smith and Tweddle. However, Stephen Greenbury does make the statement that justifies a substantial portion of this chapter: "It follows from the developers' criteria that it is virtually impossible to foresee the specific requirements of such tenants". I do not accept this. The truth of the matter is more likely to be that no-one in the industry has really ever bothered to try to find out.

6.2. The role of market research

Market research can reduce business risk by providing information on specific markets or marketing problems: over 70% of companies in the United States have formal market research departments and managers as part of their organisation. In this country most consumer companies have their own departments or buy research services from market research agencies. A recent trend has been the growth of market research in the industrial goods industry, where many consumer techniques have been shown to be capable of adaptation to more difficult and fragmented markets.

There are currently over 30 different market research activities of which the following 10 are listed by Kotler as being the most common:

(a) Determination of market characteristics.
(b) Measurement of market potentials.
(c) Market-share analysis.
(d) Sales analysis.
(e) Studies of business trends.
(f) Competitive-product studies.
(g) Short-range forecasting.
(h) New-product acceptance and potential.
(i) Long-range forecasting.
(j) Pricing studies.

It can be seen that three of these, namely (b), (g) and (i), are concerned with assessments of demand as covered in Chapter 4. The others deal with various key aspects and are applicable in one form or another to the property profession. The developer in particular has much to gain by the utilisation of these research facilities, with his own in-house expertise having an important input. In recent years the cost and apparent effectiveness of advertising has enticed many research agencies to concentrate their services in this area. Advertising "tracking" studies and the study of relationships between advertising campaigns and sales have been very much in evidence in the food industry for example.

The value of proper market research to the property world seems to have been overlooked completely and there may be three reasons for this. Firstly, surveyors and valuers are unsure of the subject: it is significant that the RICS examination syllabus does not mention market research. Secondly, property professionals, especially developers, feel that effective research will be costly, yet they will spend large amounts of money on the unfocused promotion of schemes without any real idea of who they are aiming at or what the consumer really wants. Thirdly, many people involved in property claim to know all about the market and do not need outside

Market Research

assistance. A clear indictment of this myopic attitude comes from the profession itself when it criticises the inability of developers, agents and others to "react to the needs of high-technology users"[5]. A good market research department would have identified and anticipated the potential market for industrial property developers among new high-technology companies.

Other factors standing in the way of a greater use of market research in general have been identified by Kotler:

(i) *A narrow conception* — Research seen only as a fact-finding operation without clear problem definition.

(ii) *Variable calibre of research staff* — In some companies research staff are paid at clerical levels, in others at senior executive levels, thus affecting the professionalism and value of the work.

(iii) *Late results* — Unrealistic allocation of time to undertake detailed research.

(iv) *Occasional erroneous findings* — Research will provide only tentative findings or trends, not conclusive evidence. Low budget allocation can also produce insufficient data.

(v) *Intellectual differences* — The intellectual conflict between researchers, often accused of unreality, and line-managers who want realistic, actionable data.

All this has unfortunately contributed to bring about a rather erroneous view of the value of market research by many companies, especially at a time when circumstances dictate a reduction in overheads. Yet market information is crucial to commercial success — it is the raw material of marketing.

6.3. Market research procedure.

There are generally five steps in the setting-up and operation of a market research project, all applicable to the property industry:

Defining objectives

First describe the research objectives or the subject to be investigated. Clear direction of research activity is required here to ensure that the results required come from the right target market and that sufficient valid data is obtained.

Designing the research methodology

Decisions must be taken to decide the most appropriate method of obtaining the data. These can be selected from a number of well-tried techniques:

(i) "Desk" research — the study of in-house and published information.

(ii) Observation — Attempts to learn about problems by observation.
(iii) Survey research — The technique that involves obtaining information direct from members of the target market via the following methods:
   (a) face-to-face interviews, in the home or office — a very effective method.
   (b) pre-paid self-completing questionnaires sent and returned by post (currently a bit ineffective in this country).
   (c) Interviewing by telephone — particularly useful for rapid work requiring only limited investigations.
   (d) Group discussions. This involves gathering groups of experts or "opinion leaders" together to discuss markets under the direction of a trained group leader, often a psychologist — a valuable method for research into pricing.

These techniques require skill, experience and a strong communicative ability as well as a good understanding of the subject matter. Surveyors and valuers should not fall into the trap of believing that their professional qualifications and perceived knowledge of the market mean that they are automatically accomplished researchers.

Sampling

Costs will prevent the wide coverage of target markets, forcing most research programmes to utilise samples. Large samples obviously give more reliable data, but the degree of accuracy required must be related to the amount of budget allocated. Many research projects start with a pilot survey, which not only evaluates procedure, research design and response, but also facilitates a check on sampling method.

Random sampling is both safe from bias and easy to administer. (The problem with the self-completing questionnaire mentioned earlier is that results are automatically biased, as returned questionnaires cannot be truly random.) Structured sampling or non-random methods have also been designed by research practitioners to achieve maximum statistical reliability from results at minimum cost.

Fieldwork

The collection of the data using the techniques described above is generally sub-contracted to a research or fieldwork agency, who will use trained interviewers or executives depending upon the complexity of the project. Good supervision and monitoring is necessary to ensure that the fieldwork is completed accurately, without bias and on time. Surveyors must remember, however, that market research involves people, not machines, and is, therefore, subject to swift change of circumstances. This is especially true in the industrial area, where interview appointments with senior management are always subject to the demands of the interviewee's company and not the research programme.

Data analysis

Analytical techniques can vary from a simple summation and averaging excercise to multiple regression analysis: it all depends upon the objectives of the research and the use to which the results will be put. Property professionals commissioning research services would do best to take advice from the research agency during the design stage.

Presentation of report

The results of the research and any conclusions arising should be clearly shown in a comprehensive report that will receive wide circulation in the practice. The next step is to translate the findings into action.

6.4. Implications for the property profession.

Although market research can provide the surveyor with a tool by which other parts of the property market jigsaw can be fitted together, it will never replace the role played by instinct or "gut" feel and should be viewed as an extra weapon in the battle of eliminating risk and confirming judgments. Market research adds an unknown dimension to other sources of traditional marketing intelligence.

I feel that the submission of development proposals to funding institutions in particular would benefit from more use of focused market research by the professional practice. The ability to be able to present a proposal containing evidence of user requirements, demand estimates, pricing levels and so on would give the presenters a competitive edge and impress the fund. A summary of competitive developments and their implications is also a good way to establish credibility. A point must come at which the fund's requirements for "flexibility" in a particular scheme design are either supported or refuted by market research evidence which has been compiled, analysed and interpreted by the surveyor.

Those property professionals involved in the formulation of economic and development strategies will also see the necessity of effective market research. Here the concern will be with forecasting both demand and the specific requirements of tomorrow's industrial and commercial activities. Detailed study of future economic trends, and technological developments, together with national and local government's political or social objectives, will be critical to medium and long-term strategic planning.

Market research will play its role by providing input at various stages of the process. The research manager would be asked to compile factual evidence to answer such questions as:

"After fibre-optics, what is the next major development in telecommunications and how will this affect building design?"

"What are the long-term implications of micro-technology for office developments?"

"Evaluate the feasibility of medical science parks."

"What are the long-term implications of transport policy on local and city-centre shopping developments?"

The growth of management scientists in industry has led to the development of marketing models, which are proving very valuable in such research areas as new-product development, competitive pricing, and advertising effectiveness. It is felt that the role played by models will increase in modern marketing and at some stage in the future they will, I am sure, have a place in economic and development planning.

Despite the rather depressing picture painted of the property industry's involvement in market research so far in this chapter, certain property organisations have begun to incorporate the science into their business activities. In 1982 Richard Ellis's research department published a report on the *Impact of the Microchip on the Demand for Offices*[6]; *Property and Technology — The Needs of Modern Industry*[7] was published by Herring Son & Daw following market research undertaken by planning consultants Conran Roche; and, on a similar theme, Drivers Jonas produced a research report entitled *A Review of Science Parks and High-technology Developments*[8].

The Centre for Advanced Land Use Studies (CALUS) continues to publish useful technical reports that have implications for the marketing surveyor — *Buildings for Industry* in 1979[9] and *Property and the Needs of New Technology* in 1983[10]. A seminar was organised by CALUS earlier this year on "Marketing Commercial Property". Although concentrating on promotion in the form of advertising, press and public relations rather than the wider aspects of marketing, the seminar did include a brief but inadequate paper on market research.

However, the ultimate use of research in the property world in general must be by the Barratt organisation. Scorned by many as being too aggressive, Barratt have built an effective and dynamic marketing organisation which must be the envy of many consumer companies. Market research is an integral part of their organisation. Recognising, for example, that average ages within specific target markets will rise over the next decade, Barratt's marketing team will be researching this change to identify new opportunities. As their marketing manager, Mike Norton, said in a May 1983 issue of *Marketing*[11], "market research is a continuous process".

All these moves toward the use of research are extremely sound and very healthy for the property industry, but let us not lose sight of the fact that there are enormous strides still to be made among many large and reputable organisations if success is to be achieved. The introduction of Barratt Commercial this year could be both a threat and a challenge to the established commercial agents in this country.

6.5 The use of a research agency

Lack of time, as much as a lack of expertise, will inevitably prevent most professional practices from undertaking market research using their in-house staff. Besides which, the techniques involved preclude surveyors or valuers from proper research work; their contribution is valuable instead in respect of expert opinion and "gut" feel. A practice does, however, require a marketing professional in order to control any research projects commissioned by the firm or its clients. I consider this to be essential before research of any kind is contemplated. If a practice does not have a marketer on its staff, then I strongly recommend the use of an independent marketing consultant to control research.

Research agencies fall into five main groups in this country:

Fieldwork agencies

Companies in this group will undertake fieldwork in any part of the United Kingdom, given sample details, questionnaires and a timescale. A fixed-fee arrangement is advisable to control costs. Some fieldwork agencies are capable of undertaking sample and questionnaire design, analysis and reporting.

Consumer agencies

These agencies specialise in researching consumer markets. Many sub-contract fieldwork to a fieldwork agency, which is an acceptable arrangement if no "mark-up" of fees is involved. Major consumer research agencies will offer a range of services such as product testing, group discussions, packaging research, etc. Fees can be agreed on a fixed basis with most of them, so do not deal with an agency that will not negotiate a fixed-fee arrangement. All reputable consumer agencies are members of the Market Research Society.

Industrial agencies

Industrial markets, which are often fragmented and internationally spread, require a technical approach and researchers who can learn technology quickly. Most of the work involves considerable desk research and in-depth direct interviewing techniques. Fees can be agreed on a "per valid interview" basis, typically £100 to £300 each at present. Agencies of worth are members of the Industrial Marketing Research Association.

Specialist agencies

Economic circumstances and new markets have produced a number of specialist agencies covering such aspects as:
— Pricing
— Telephone interviewing
— Advertising effectiveness
— Tourism
— Syndicated research
— New product development
— Trade research.

There are currently no research agencies specialising in the property market other than the Property Research Team, a division of Retail Audits Ltd based in Newport, Gwent.

Consultants

A number of groups, comprising planners, economists and management consultants, are currently offering market research services, especially in the new industrial technology areas. Beware of these, as many do not have the necessary expertise! Furthermore, unlike agencies, many consultants are not members of the Market Research Society or the Industrial Marketing Research Association and are therefore not bound by codes of conduct which protect interviewees from, for example, direct-selling activities disguised as market research.

6.6. An example

Let us assume that a developer is contemplating a major shopping/office scheme in a provincial town. He would probably compile the data outlined by Cadman and Austin-Crowe in the form of an inventory of published information. The market viability of the scheme would depend heavily upon "gut" feel and historical data provided by local commercial agents. The project would be drawn up and presented to planners and funds to seek approval and finance. Once agreed, acquisition and construction would probably start well before any thought was given to promotion of the scheme to potential tenants.

Figure 11 shows the role that market research could have played in the working-up of the scheme to produce hard evidence and information to improve marketability. A research agency, preferably with an industrial base, as this is more suited to property markets, would be commissioned to undertake sample interviews among existing office businesses in the catchment area. Some idea of current demand and design requirements could then be obtained. Next, desk research would assimilate all the data in an attempt to forecast future demand. A consumer agency could then undertake fieldwork among existing shoppers to establish patterns, perceptions and desires of the consumers. I would not rule out the possibility of interviewing property managers of multi-national retail companies to test the scheme concept, although there is a limit to their involvement at this stage.

The promotional strategy for the scheme would draw heavily upon the results of each area of research, which would have identified target sectors and how best to approach them. The data would also enable the developer and agent to establish a competitive position by seeking an edge over other schemes in the area. This might be based upon price, design, quality or special deals. Further periodic research would be necessary to update the original work, monitor lettings and, most importantly, to identify in advance any changes in the market place by either competitor or consumer that would affect the competitive position of the scheme. Defensive action could then be taken.

Chapter 6. References.

[1] "Marketing Management — Analysis, Planning and Control". Philip Kotler. Prentice/Hall International. 1980.
[2] "Property Development". David Cadman and Leslie Austin-Crowe. SPON. 1983.
[3] United States Industrial Development Handbook 1980. Urban Land Institute.
[4] "The Practice of Estate Agency" Nigel Stephens. The Estates Gazette Ltd 1980.
[5] Derek Penfold. 1982 Property Review. "Estates Gazette". January 22nd 1983.
[6] "The Impact of the Microchip on the Demand for Offices". Richard Ellis. 1982.
[7] "Property and Technology — The Needs of Modern Industry". Herring Son & Daw. 1982.
[8] "A Review of Science Parks and High-Technology Developments". Drivers Jonas. 1982.
[9] "Building for Industry". Centre for Advanced Land Use Studies 1979.
[10] "Property and the Needs of New Technology". Centre for Advanced Land Use Studies 1983.
[11] Mike Norton. "Marketing". May 1983.

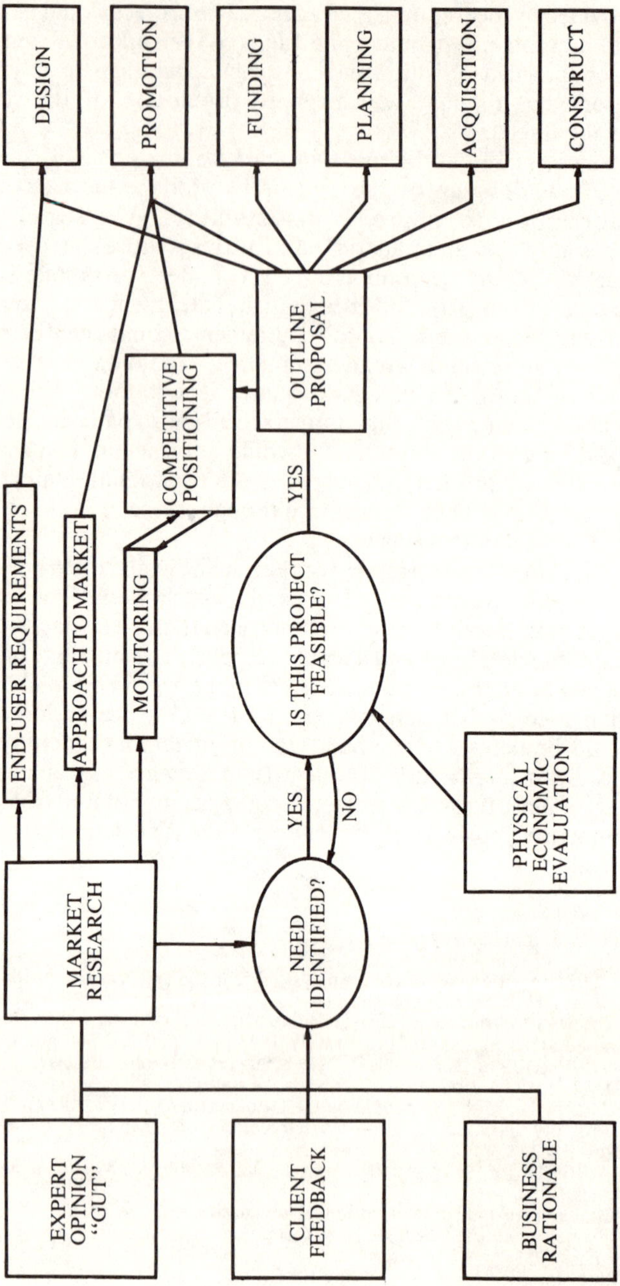

Figure 11 The role of market research in development appraisal

CHAPTER 7
Market Segmentation and Targeting

This chapter deals with the relatively new theory of market segmentation, which has been born from the inability of consumer and industrial companies to satisfy large complex markets with products often involving substantial promotional support at a time when all costs are under severe review. The marketing surveyor or valuer can learn from the use of this technique, in respect of both property disposal and the marketing of the practice.

The need for the consideration of these essential elements in the property marketing armoury is apparent from recent events. The oversupply of commercial and industrial property in the United Kingdom has prompted only a casual glance at segmentation and targeting, with most agents still hoping that a "shotgun" approach, covering wide markets, will produce lettings. The problem is exacerbated by the range and quality of second-hand property on the market and the continued insistence by the funding institutions on total design "flexibility". Offices and shops tend to fare better than industrial buildings, since by definition they are usually designed to suit certain market segments. However, the advent of specialised micro-technology R and D operations has called into question the design of industrial space, as office-style developments seem better suited to the needs of some consumers.

The *Estates Gazette* property review of 1982[1] contained several pointers that a marketer would recognise as resulting from a lack of segmentation analysis. In the prologue, Derek Penfold referred to developers and agents jumping on the high-tech bandwagon by painting-up old premises. This in turn led to consumer cynicism in a year when the prospective tenant demanded more. As Penfold says, "tenants are becoming increasingly sophisticated in their requirements" — a suggestion that market segmentation among some potential customers may be possible.

It is in the area of high-technology and science parks that confusion of target markets by agents seems to set in. Aztec-West in Bristol is seen by one agent as a possible "blue-print" for all high-technology developments geared to a rapidly changing market. This would seem to suggest that the product has been researched and designed for the high-tech segment of the market which is a huge and complex market by any standards. Certainly, the literature for the scheme seems to suggest that specific targets have been identified. The other letting agent, however, refers to Aztec-West as a development able to provide a storage and distribution centre (because of the proximity to a motorway junction), offices (minutes away from an inter-city railway station), production space (easy access to the centre of Bristol), or a combination of all three! In other words, a typically traditional, high-headroom, mixed development with trees, called a "high-technology development", "business park" or whatever, where a double-glazing contractor could be accommodated next to a food distribution centre on one side and an electronics assembly outfit on the other.

The agents find themselves, of course, in a difficult position, where their ambitions for, say, a science park scheme, based upon experience and knowledge, are frustrated by the funding institutions' reluctance to back such developments. This attitude is likely to continue, in my view, until such times as the agent's presentation of a development proposal contains convincing market evidence, including segmentation analysis and targeting proposals. Some funds have expressed strong interest in evaluating special developments such as science parks (they are already funding distribution centres). Sun Alliance and Commercial Union are but two, although they clearly require a slant which suggests that some clear thought has been given to the "market" viability of the scheme, not simply that "it is a good site".

Cambridge Science Park appears to be more focused than others and has attracted over 25 companies involved in broad scientific activities. This degree of exclusivity, however, does not appear to have been achieved by positive marketing but rather by a combination of effective management and snobbery. One has the feeling that taking space at Cambridge is similar to seeking membership of an exclusive London club. This may be a successful approach in a situation where the demand from specific sub-sectors of the market exceeds or equals the supply of premises in a location adjacent to a university, such as Cambridge. I do not believe, however, that such apparent success can be sustained or repeated elsewhere in the United Kingdom, where the range of choice and hard commercial reality are factors which agents have to cope with every day.

7.1. Market segmentation

The task of segmentation can be described as the identification of a

Market Segmentation and Targeting

group of consumers inside a market who share a common need. It is essential to qualify this by remembering that that need will change in accord with the marketing and economic environment and is therefore subject to change by external influences. It is also possible to create a common need, such as in the case of video-cassette recorders, as well as influence it.

Segmentation also identifies those variables that are used in the purchase decision and, most importantly, ranks them in order of importance by means of market research plus a good measure of expert and salesforce opinion. This is especially valuable in the property industry, where the collective experience of the professional practice or developer should be exploited in the segmentation analysis.

A term commonly used for the segmentation activity is "gap analysis", aptly describing the market-opportunity analysis undertaken continuously by marketing-orientated companies. The work enables the marketer to identify gaps in the market which, given sufficient resources, the company can fill. A better understanding of particular markets can also be achieved enabling the company to exploit the opportunity by well-focused targeting. For example, it is generally assumed that extensive landscaping is an occupier requirement on science parks and much is made of it by both the developer and his agent. Segmentation analysis would first establish the relative importance of landscaping as a purchase decision variable and would then identify the form and ranking of other key variables. It may be that for a particular segment of the market, landscaping is a strong variable, while for other segments the availability of a built-in gas network is a more important variable. The developer then decides whether or not to aim for this segment as a prime target, either because there is a market gap or because he feels that his competitive positioning will enable him to take a chunk of his competitors' market share.

The total market for the commercial property surveyor or valuer is made up of industrial and consumer companies, service industries, professional practices, government departments, "quangos", retailers, local authorities and so on. Their common need is that they all require buildings and expert advisory services on property matters. It is important to recognise that other common needs may be shared by all or part of the total market and that differing "preferences" will emerge in the purchasing decision of certain segments.

Most markets break down into what is termed "preference segments". There are three of these and although each is fairly wide they do represent the first step in segmentation analysis based upon "product" attributes.

(1) *Homogenous preferences* — where all consumers in the market have roughly the same preferences. Most companies would position their product "in the middle", hoping to cater for the majority of consumers in that market.

(2) *Diffused preferences* — Consumer preferences are scattered with each requiring something different from the product. Companies often decide to position in the middle to minimise consumer dissatisfaction. (Political parties tend to do this.)

(3) *Clustered preferences* — Distinct clusters are in evidence suggesting further segmentation. The company must decide which of the following courses of action to follow in order to achieve its objectives:

   (i) Undifferentiated marketing. Position in the centre to appeal to most groups.
   (ii) Concentrated marketing. Position in the biggest cluster and try to become market leader (Barratt Homes, for example).
   (iii) Differentiated marketing. Develop several "brands" to cover each cluster.

This analysis applies equally to industrial, consumer or other markets and can be quite accurately assessed by the two main inputs, market research and expert opinion. The commercial and industrial property developer or his agent has to undertake this exercise as a first step in segmentation analysis. While potential tenants for shops and offices follow a fairly homogenous pattern, the market for industrial floorspace probably breaks down into clustered preferences, with different groups of consumers preferring different "product" (premises) attributes.

Another interesting segmentation analysis concerns the residential seller/buyer market in terms of the attributes of the residential agency practice. Attempts to break into the market or expand operations to another area would benefit greatly from this kind of analytical approach, especially if it is the firm's intention to exploit any untapped market potential. How is this comprised? What do people expect from a residential agency (preference analysis)? Is there a gap that can be filled?

Mass markets such as this are capable of segmentation. Louis Boone and David Kurtz in their book *Contemporary Marketing*[2] quote as an example toothpaste, which is used by every consumer, and yet striped toothpaste was developed for children, Crest focuses on prevention of tooth decay and Ultra-Brite hints at enhanced sex appeal. I have stated before that the marketing of property is more closely allied to the marketing of industrial rather than consumer products, and so it is with the further stages of segmentation.

Yoram Wind and Richard Cardozo identified in 1974[3] the characteristics that make up the segmentation of industrial markets and I have listed those which I feel are applicable to property:

Macrosegments
— product application
— customer size
— geographical location
— structure of the organisation

Microsegments
— position in company
— personal characteristics
— perceived product importance
— attitudes towards vendor (agent)
— buying decision criteria
— stage in buying process

Clearly, there are many ways to segment a market right down to groups of individuals. It is essential, however, to remember that to be viable market segments should have three main characteristicts. Kotler[4] describes them as:

(a) Measureability — The degree to which the size and purchasing power of segments can be measured. Some will be hard to measure, thus introducing a level of uncertainty in the strategic decision.

(b) Accessibility — The degree to which the segments can be effectively reached and served.

(c) Substantiality — The degree to which the size and purchasing power of the segment makes it worthwhile for the company to give it special marketing attention (ie to target). This will also depend upon the size and style of the developer or agent, his competitive strengths, etc.

To summarise, there are three main aspects of the benefits of segmentation for the surveyor or valuer. Firstly, the surveyor or his practice is in a better position to spot and compare market opportunities. Secondly, marketing programmes and the promotional campaigns contained within them can be more effectively aimed. Thirdly, resources can be more effectively allocated by being geared to the response characteristics of the different market segments.

7.2. Targeting

Having segmented the market into identifiable and viable pieces, the practice now has to decide which segment can be profitably targeted, based upon the choice of marketing options available, as described above. In practice, characteristics of the developer or his agent, the product (ie location and planning control), as well as the market itself, will tend to constrain the actual choice of a target marketing strategy. As far as property is concerned, the following would seem to be constraints:

(a) The resources of the company or practice. Financial resources may restrict the implementation of a target marketing strategy and one must not forget the level of priority given to such activities by the current property practitioners.

(b) The stage reached in the product life cycle (discussed in Chapter 4). The point may be reached where no funds would be allocated for a targeting exercise.

(c) Market homogeneity. In markets where buyers' tastes are broadly the same as in office or shop development, an undifferentiated marketing strategy would be more appropriate, facilitating targeting on a broad sector of the market.

(d) Competitors' marketing strategies. Active segmentation by competitors makes it hard for firms to practice undifferentiated marketing. Conversely, as property developers and agents all seem to be implementing this particular strategy at present, then the person who practices active segmentation and focused targeting could gain.

Once target markets are identified, plans can be formulated to approach and attack that market: that is the marketing "mix". Objectives must be laid down and a minimum level of achievement agreed by management and staff to be reached within an acceptable budget and timescale.

Previous chapters have dealt with demand measurement and forecasting, which are often undertaken as part of segmentation analysis. The next chapter deals with the promotional planning required to communicate with the target sector.

7.3. Implications for the surveyor

Clearly there is a new role in segmentation and targeting for the market-orientated surveyor and his practice. I believe that this will be the next major step in better marketing planning in a number of different industries, including property development.

Segmentation analysis should form part of the development appraisal process by providing data that will influence location, design, costs and hence commercial viability of schemes aimed at specific target markets. The exercise can never be a once-only activity, simply because markets are dynamic and not static.

Even in the United States, segmentation analysis has not yet fully become part of the development process, although references are made to analytical activities during the appraisal stage. The 1980 *US Industrial Development Handbook*[5] refers to market analysis, which is described as the analysis of factors to establish the potential for industrial growth and development. It adds that "this information will also be used to identify the types of industrial users or investors which constitute the most likely sources of demand for space within a development". In a reference to sales brochures, the handbook says that they should contain "a synopsis of community characteristics drawn from the market analysis studies" — almost a market segmentation exercise, but not quite, because the writer assumes that demand exists and can be reliably forecast using such parameters as employment projections. The American developer then sets his sights on obtaining a share of this growth rather than a share of his competitors' market, which could be declining rather than growing.

In the United Kingdom, and I suspect latterly in the United States, property markets are not growing in most areas or within most market segments. New developments are chasing decreasing or static markets, others are pitching into the growing new-technology sector by providing science and business parks, innovation centres etc, without any clear idea of market characteristics, to the point where saturation and then oversupply seems imminent. Yet we find many new-technology companies cynical about premises provided for them and agents having different views of the objectives of new development schemes.

Now is the time for the innovative marketing-committed practice to make a killing. Market gaps do exist, potential is measurable and new markets can be gained by the entrepenurial practice.

Chapter 7. References.

[1] The Estates Gazette Property Review 1982. January 22nd 1983.
[2] "Contemporary Marketing". Louis E. Boone and David L. Kurtz. The Dryden Press. Illinois. 1977.
[3] "Industrial Market Segmentation". Yoram Wind and Richard Cardozo. Industrial Marketing Management. 1974.
[4] "Marketing Management, Analysis, Planning and Control". Philip Kotler. Prentice/Hall International 1980.
[5] "United States Industrial Development Handbook 1980". Urban Land Institute.

CHAPTER 8
Promotion

Promotion, or the art of communicating with prospective customers, is a vital component of the marketing mix. What this term actually covers depends both upon the nature of the company and its products, together with characteristics of the target markets identified as being capable of producing business. Although basic methods of communication with customers remain the same for virtually all targets and across most products, emphasis on individual activities will obviously vary widely.

The purpose of promotion is simply to bring a product or service to the attention of a buyer, or group of buyers, in the target market. In the property profession there is a great deal of confusion about the meaning of promotion, the most common error in my experience being the use of the term "marketing" instead of "promotion". Promotion includes selling as one of its constituent parts, but is an activity under the marketing umbrella. I have chosen to treat selling and the operation of a salesforce separately in Chapter 9 because of the implications for the property profession.

Another error is the use of "marketing" instead of "advertising". Again, advertising is a component of promotion but attracts much attention because of cost and because many commercial agents believe it to be the only way to communicate with the customer. Recent attempts by various property-related organisations, such as CALUS, in sponsoring badly-focused seminars have done little to dispel these myths in the minds of the surveyor and valuer.

It is worth repeating at this stage the definition of marketing, which is to "identify, anticipate and satisfy consumer requirements at a profit". Promotion, or communication, is to do with the *satisfaction* element that will be achieved by presenting the product to the market place, the product itself having been developed as a result of the *identification* of consumer need. The timing of the promotion will be based upon the *anticipation* of that need.

Promotion, then, can be seen to include a number of communicative elements which are generally considered to be:

Advertising
  Press
  Television
  Radio
  Posters (signboards)
Public Relations
  Press
  Public
  Sponsorship
Direct selling (salesforce)
Direct mail (mailshots)
Exhibitions
Literature
Film and audio visual
Conferences and seminars
Packaging and presentation
Gifts and novelties
Special events

The effectiveness of each of these must be related to cost and to the markets in which the firm is operating. I have mentioned previously that the marketing of commercial and industrial property is more akin to industrial than consumer products, and I feel that this can be borne out in promotional terms by a consideration of the nature of the "consumer" of industrial and commercial property as opposed to the consumer of residential property. The decision to purchase property invariably rests with a buyer group rather than an individual (or husband and wife). The group may comprise a full board, a top management team or, in the case of a small business, a couple of partners who may perhaps need the approval of their bank manager. The segmentation analysis described in Chapter 7 may have identified each group.

Unlike the consumer mass market, which must include most house purchasers, the industrial market is fragmented, requiring a greater emphasis on direct selling techniques. This is where the professional salesman becomes a true asset. Purchasers of industrial and commercial property also tend to be "high information seekers" whether they are members of a buyer group, or decision-making unit, or reporting to the board with recommendations. High information seekers are common in markets where the product is expensive, risky or purchased infrequently. Industrial and commercial premises would fall into this category both for the large company contemplating a new plant or the small business seeking industrial space to rent. Either decision involves an expensive risk in relative terms.

Direct selling is one communicative method that guarantees the provision of detailed information, whereas advertising does not. Yet here we find another misconception. The purpose of advertising is not necessarily to provide detailed information but to attract attention and to persuade the consumer to seek additional information. The readers of *Estates Gazette* may not view the property pages as dispassionately as is sometimes claimed. Otherwise, why bother with full-page colour advertising? Why not simply list properties available in a simple classified format?

The effectiveness of the various methods of promotion in both the consumer and industrial markets is well illustrated in figure 12, which shows the relative weight of each method in those markets. It can be seen that advertising plays less of a role than direct selling in the promotion of industrial goods. Figure 13 shows the relevance of each method in the actual purchase decision. Again, advertising plays a lesser role than direct selling.

I use these diagrams to emphasise two points. First, that advertising is more effective in consumer, rather than industrial, markets and secondly that where advertising does achieve results it is in creating awareness. If the assumption about similarities between the industrial goods market and the commercial and industrial property market is correct, then the use and value of consumer-style advertising to promote property must be questioned.

The first step in promotional planning is to design a strategy by

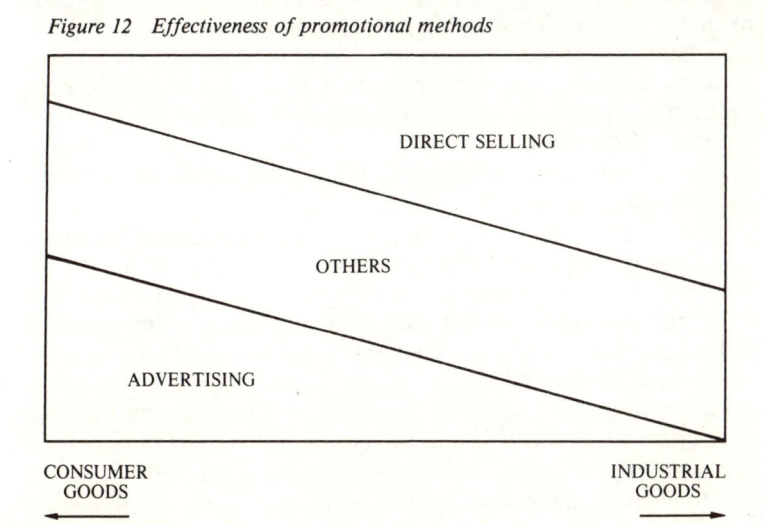

Figure 12 Effectiveness of promotional methods

Figure 13 *Effectiveness of promotional methods at buyer readiness stages*

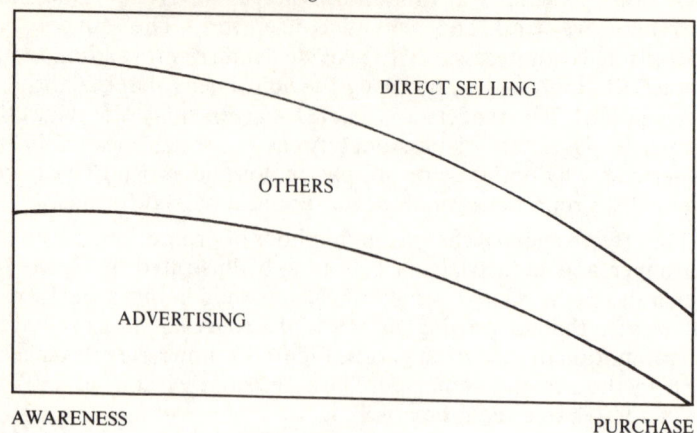

```
                                    DIRECT SELLING

                         OTHERS


              ADVERTISING

AWARENESS                                        PURCHASE
```

which each technique will be cost-effectively used to communicate with the target market. While various methods may be tried and evaluated over a time, there is an overriding need for an integrated approach. It is both wasteful and largely ineffective to try the various communicative methods one by one, expecting that each try will produce better results than the previous method. This uncoordinated approach is both amateurish and expensive.

A promotional strategy sets out the objectives to be achieved, the timescale allowed and the budget allocated. It is a simple statement of intent from which a number of communicative tasks will flow. The detailed schedule of tasks must be designed so as to maximise available resources and to take account of any seasonal influences. This activity schedule is best organised on a time basis, say over 12 months, where the effect of the winter season or summer holiday period can be catered for or exploited, depending upon the nature of the task.

My own views on the effectiveness of each promotional method for the property profession are given in this chapter and I fully accept that many experienced surveyors will have different views based upon successes in the past. Nevertheless, it is important to remember that markets are dynamic, not static, and a successful method today may be inappropriate tomorrow. Market research, expert opinion and salesforce feedback will provide the marketer with up-to-date information for his promotional planning.

Each target market will have its own quirks but I would recommend an integrated approach along the following lines for promoting, for example, a science park to a target sector in the electronics market. It is assumed that the market research and segmentation analysis has been completed and that the building design and mix reflect the findings.

The target group is divided not only by industrial activity but also by "buyer stages". An appreciation of the value of various promotional methods at each buyer stage enables the marketer to plan the campaign logically and cost-effectively and to avoid wasteful expenditure at inappropriate stages:

Buyer stage	*Promotional Activity*
Awareness	Advertising (trade press)
	Press editorial
Comprehension	Literature
	Exhibitions
	Special events
Conviction	Direct selling
	Advertising (signboards)
	Site visits
Purchase	Direct selling
	Public Relations (to build credibility)

Note, however, that the activities listed will not be implemented in strict succession but will overlap. It is essential to integrate these activities on a time schedule.

Figure 14 shows the promotional plan geared to the construction programme for the scheme. It is assumed that the first hint that a new scheme is planned occurs during the research phase undertaken prior to scheme design. In this simple example, care is taken to ensure that the announcement of the scheme through awareness advertising during months 1 and 2 coincides with the design phase and that a simple brochure called a "flyer" is available to generate initial interest. The value of the scheme as a new development is exploited by using press editorial during the "awareness" phase in month 2.

Subsequent advertising during month 5 is designed to include, for example, photographs of a model of the development to explain the scheme visually and to invite requests for information. Editorial bursts coincide with exhibitions to sustain interest.

"Special events" may include a design party, probably with commercial agents and possibly bankers as guests, in month 4 and an on-site launch ceremony at the end of construction in month 12. Also programmed are a series of site visits during the "comprehension" and "conviction" phases. These should only be arranged for genuine enquirers or those persons who will promote the scheme as third

108 *The Marketing of Industrial and Commercial Property*

Figure 14 Promotional Plan for a new Development Scheme

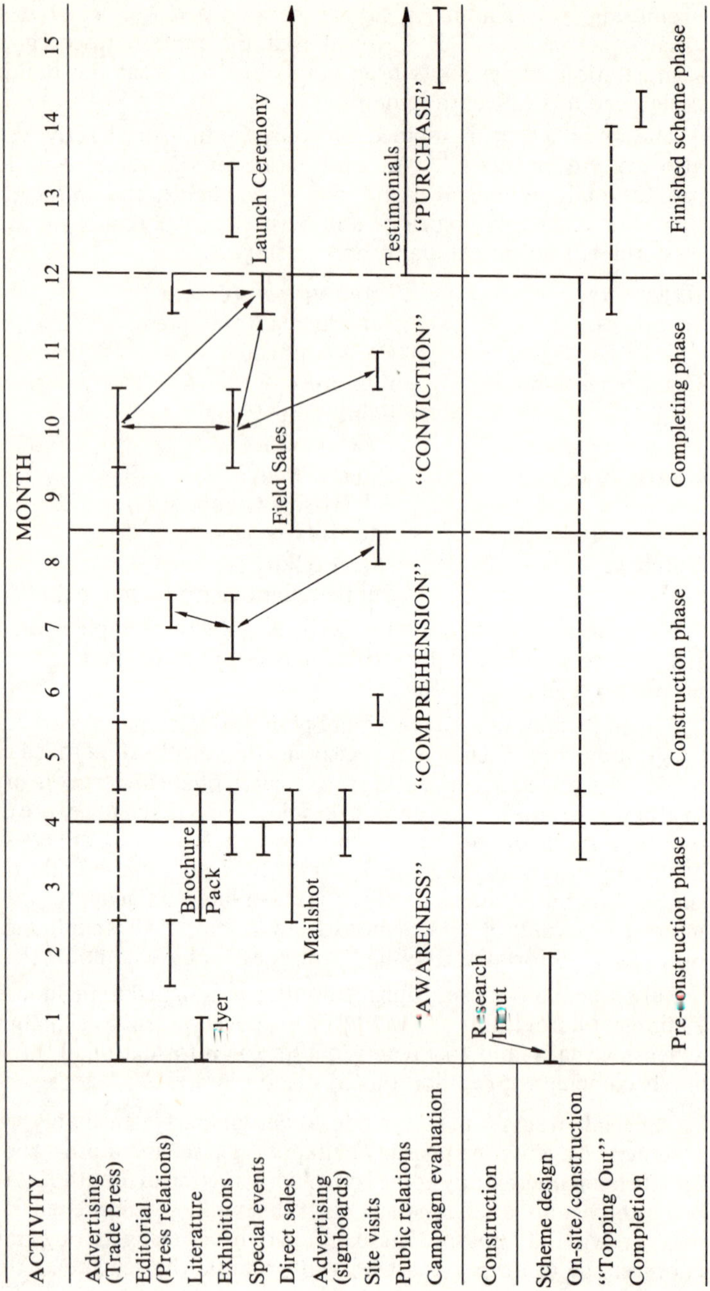

ACTIVITY	MONTH
Advertising (Trade Press)	
Editorial (Press relations)	
Literature	Flyer / Brochure Pack
Exhibitions	
Special events	Mailshot / Launch Ceremony
Direct sales	Field Sales
Advertising (signboards)	
Site visits	
Public relations	Testimonials
Campaign evaluation	"AWARENESS" — "COMPREHENSION" — "CONVICTION" — "PURCHASE"
Construction	Research /Input
Scheme design	
On-site/construction	
"Topping Out"	
Completion	Pre-construction phase / Construction phase / Completing phase / Finished scheme phase

parties, for example, property journalists. Site visits during months 8 and 11 may have been instigated by exhibitions in which the scheme was promoted during months 7 and 10.

A targeted mailshot with telephone follow-up would be undertaken during months 3 and 4 but intensive activity by the sales team may not need to start until month 9, picking up any leads generated by that time. Public and press relations activity is used from month 12 onwards to inform the target market that the scheme is letting "as planned" or "better than anticipated" or whatever. New tenants are involved in this particular activity to help establish credibility and to provide further sales leads among their own business contacts. The owner or developers may consider sponsoring the first occupier of the scheme as a public relations exercise, perhaps in the form of a competition to find the most enterprising new product in this sector.

In the professional practice, a number of promotional strategies would be developed during a typical year, each one aimed at promoting a particular development to a particular target market.

The development of a promotional strategy for the practice itself is also an important part of the marketer's job, and the steps taken differ little from those entailed in the design of a promotional plan for a shopping centre or industrial park. The firm would have identified new markets through its opportunity analysis and segmentation activities. Decisions then need to be taken on how to establish the practice in its new location or to develop a new area of potential business. All the techniques described in this chapter are available, only the "mix" is different. One thing is certain in the industrial and commercial field: no single unsustained activity is sufficient on its own, and an integrated approach is also required to promote the practice. The plan is capable of operating under pre-determined budget and time constraints with the amount of new business or extra market share obtained being carefully monitored.

Expenditure on all these items, whether to promote a scheme or the practice itself, is covered at various points in this chapter. Costs are a critical element in promotional planning, as most agents are often faced with having to convince clients that large sums of money are necessary to promote schemes effectively.

8.1. Advertising

I have selected this promotional activity first for three reasons: firstly, to ensure that the reader understands the role advertising plays in property marketing; secondly, because advertising costs are high and, thirdly, because many consumer and industrial companies are beginning to question the effectiveness of this form of communication. Surveyors and valuers have a duty constantly to question the value of all promotional activity on behalf of their clients.

Advertising is big business in the United Kingdom with £2,562m spent in 1980 (the highest in Western Europe) of which £1,145m was press advertising. In the 10 years between 1970 and 1980, advertising costs rose by 300%, with the yearly percentage increases higher than the rise in the Retail Price Index.

Let us first consider how advertising works. The purpose of an advertisement is to communicate a selling message to a potential consumer. It is often argued that its purpose is to inform or to persuade a consumer, which is true, but both these actions are, in reality, only selling messages in different forms. Corporate advertising is the name given to that style of advertising which seeks to promote a company as being good, dependable, valuable to the community, etc, but does not say "buy this product" in a direct sense. Recent advertising on television by British Petroleum is a classic example and press advertising by public companies in the *Financial Times* is another, where the aim is to persuade shareholders that a potential take-over bid would be against the interests of the company, the country or the economy. A professional practice may well consider corporate advertising to be valuable in promoting the practice, and recent advertisements by large national practices in the *Estates Gazette* anniversary issue would fit into this category. However, most advertising within the surveyor's area of activity is concerned with the promotion of property for clients and so I will concentrate on this.

A worry that plagues all advertisers, irrespective of the product, is the effectiveness of his advertisements. Creative designers and copywriters strive to make their clients' advertisements "memorable" and yet research in the United States shows that, in certain markets, sales are only randomly related to memorability.

Consumers use what are described by Herbert Krugman, the research manager of GEC[1], as "perceptual screens", which effectively cut out sales messages unless particular information is being sought. For example, a person who has purchased a music centre will scan all advertisements prior to purchase in order to obtain information to make a judgment. He will also note music centre advertisements after purchase to justify his decision and to seek assurance that the decision was both sound and cost-effective. Research in 1970 using 47 American magazines showed that although 44% of readers claimed to have noticed a particular advertisement, only 9% read enough to identify the product brand. TV advertising research at about the same time indicated that only 12% of the viewing audience could recall advertisements from particular programmes.

Throughout the 1970s in the United Kingdom a controversy raged among experts, some claiming that there was no connection between advertisement recall and sales while admitting that an increase in "brand awareness" with any consumer must be a good thing. Recent more sophisticated research by Cadbury definitely shows a statistical relationship between advertising awareness and sales in the chocolate confectionery market. It also seems that quiet, persuasive advertisements are recalled more significantly by British consumers than brash, hard-sell advertising.

Whether persuasive advertising results in more purchases is an interesting point. Krugman claims that advertising of any kind can only capture attention or increase awareness and is unlikely to persuade consumers to purchase outright. The consumer is seeking information but only perceives that which is of interest to him at that time in that particular marketing environment. Krugman argues that advertising is "not ineffective or impotent but there is terrific competition for consumers' attention", hence the "perceptual screen".

There is one further piece of research to note before we consider the implications for the property profession. Advertising can be used to generate enquiries either by coupon, freephone or a similar device. The consumer has been made aware of the product, understands the message and now wants further information. The action of request is interpreted by many as being a "live" enquiry to be pursued. I would not disagree with this and in fact would criticise the property profession in being too slack in following up sales leads, but are all these enquiries "live"? Studies by McGraw Hill in the United States showed that about 50% of all enquirers responding to an advertising campaign were collecting data for reference, 25% would buy or were already using a competitor's product and around 12% were potential new purchasers. A low "hit" rate like this for an expensive advertising campaign reinforces previous points made about the need for careful research, segmentation and targeting, so that at least advertisements will, hopefully, be read by the right group of buyers. Clearly, spill-over exposure to the wrong target audience is both wasteful and ineffective.

The property profession seem to regard press advertising as the only real way to communicate with potential buyers of commercial and industrial premises. Three main property media are used extensively, *Estates Gazette*, *Estates Times* and *Chartered Surveyor Weekly*. These are a good choice in that a target audience has been pre-selected by the nature of the publications. A mixed readership including students, competitors (ie other agents) and non-decision makers is considered to be no bad thing. The fact that some agents are themselves "buyers" of property on behalf of their own clients is obviously also important.

It is relatively easy to put together a clever, colourful advertising campaign in any, or all three, of these publications. If sales result and *can be directly attributed to the advertisements,* then everyone is happy. If no sales result, then some excuse will always be found, such as "we need a more sustained campaign", or "we should have gone to full colour". It is too easy to attribute failure to the advertising rather than the fact that the campaign has not been properly planned. Advertising can be effective as part of an integrated promotional plan.

Let us consider the form and content of property advertisements. Too many property adverts are stereotyped with cliches and frequently more text than can be easily read quickly. Plate 13 shows a "spoof" advertisement to illustrate the point. Remember that the objective is to use persuasive memorability to create interest and awareness. Good advertisements are focused on the target market with limited factual content concentrating on the benefits that the property or scheme can offer.

I disagree with Nigel Stephens[2] who suggests that the same negotiator who prepares details should also draft advertisements. He does, however, recommend that a partner should vet all advertisements prior to publication. I agree with this but would add that the partner must also have responsibility for *all* marketing functions, and should be responsible for the work of the practice's advertising or public relations agency. I attach some importance to the last item, as the proper use of outside professional advice, be it in copywriting, creative design or media selection, is the only way to properly serve the interests of the client.

How many times should one advertise a particular property and in how many publications? Advertising agencies tend to be preoccupied with audience size rather than content and character of the media used. Evidence collected in both the United Kingdom and the United States shows a close correlation between market coverage and audience "reach". In the UK the three best publications for a target market will give about 80% coverage. A fourth publication, with the same advertisement used in the same campaign, will increase coverage by less than 5%. In the case of closely related publications such as the three property journals referred to earlier, coverage must be high with just one of them. Experiences are the same in the USA, where three publications have shown to yield 91% coverage, with five yielding only a further 2%. In fact, I would be suspicious of a media schedule that proposed more than three publications be used in one campaign.

The risk of duplication is possible when one considers the circulation of this country's three main property publications as at December 1983:

Estates Gazette	— 25,000
Estates Times	— 30,000
Chartered Surveyor Weekly	— 43,000

Apart from the fact that many practices and property departments of companies may receive all these journals, circulation is not always an indication of reach. Research has shown that the readership of the *Estates Gazette* is considerably higher than its circulation, currently about 92,000. This is very important when planning an advertising campaign. In contrast, *Time* magazine lost 14% of its readership in the United States between 1973 and 1974, but the level of paid circulation remained the same.

Readership "mix" is also critical to advertising and despite extensive research by publishing houses across a wide range of magazines and newspapers, there is no way in which the right blend of coverage and reach can be guaranteed. A proportion of the cost of advertising will be wasted but it is obviously important for the surveyor to attempt to follow some basic principles in order to reduce wastage and to make advertising cost-effective.

Many commercial agents now maintain in-house advertising departments who are responsible for copywriting, design and brochure production, perhaps with a number of other promotional responsibilities. This arrangement is generally cheaper than commissioning a full-service advertising agency, yet I feel that there is a danger of stereotyping and of stemming real innovation by maintaining in-house services. It is rare to find that the person responsible is at a partner level in a practice or has any real authority and despite often being termed "director" has no more responsibility than an advertising manager. Various design houses have arisen in the last 10 years and these can be very valuable for the creative design of advertisements. It is a mistake, however, to assume that these service companies are also experts at marketing. Despite titles such as "marketing communications consultants" or "advertising and marketing agents", these groups are themselves misunderstanding and misusing the term marketing. Having an expertise in promotion does not make you a marketing consultant.

Full-service advertising agencies can be of value to a professional practice in that creativity is a cornerstone of their expertise and many are able to obtain a better deal when buying advertising media space than a commercial property agent. They also understand the system better than a surveyor. However, it is possible to ensure that the terms of the agreement are such that the agency is retained on an annual fee basis and that media commissions are paid only to the client or the practice.

Initial discussions with an advertising agency prior to the mounting of a campaign for, say, an existing office block could follow this format:

— Who are we trying to reach?
— What is the size of the (target) audience?
— What are the deciding factors (competitive edge) that will make companies buy or lease this office as opposed to any other office?
— What do we want to communicate to our prospects?
— Which of the media will do the best job at lowest cost?
— How many of the audience already know or believe the basic message?
— How are we to measure results?

This disciplinary procedure is, in effect, an expansion of the task method described earlier and will ensure the logical approach to advertising planning so often missing from current practice.

Before leaving advertising, it is useful to consider the findings of research undertaken in Europe and reported by Professor Lambin from the University of Louvain[3]. In referring to industrial goods, the parallel with property in my opinion, Professor Lambin believes that advertising complements other activities in the communications mix. A point echoed in the *Harvard Business Review* by Derek Newton[4] who reports that it has been demonstrated that advertising and "sales promotion" together produce higher sales than either alone, yet in many companies "they are considered separately and independently". "Sales promotion", in this sense, means the group of activities other than advertising. Professor Lambin was able to draw a number of conclusions from his research:

(a) Advertising effectiveness can be understood (or explained) only in relation to the total communications mix.
(b) Advertising has a limited capacity to *stimulate* market growth.
(c) Advertising is powerful only when accompanied by other promotional activities.

(d) Advertising content is more important than the amount of money spent.
(e) In non-expandable markets (property in 1983?) increased advertising expenditure "hurts" the consumer by unnecessarily escalating costs, which have to be met. (The consumer benefits only from better quality and cheaper prices in these markets.)
(f) Industrial buying behaviour is more rational than has been assumed.
(g) Factual and informative advertising is both welcomed and more effective than persuasive advertising.

8.2. Public relations

Public relations, or PR for short, has become a catch-all phrase for a number of promotional activities, including the arrangement of "free" advertising. The use of PR has grown in this country to the point where specialists now exist as PR consultants in their own right, whereas previously the activities were generally undertaken as part of the normal work of an advertising agency.

Norman Hart[5] maintains that public relations is separate from press relations in that the former is concerned with projecting the company image to opinion influencers, government or any other group likely to have an effect upon the company's future. By contrast, Philip Kotler groups both activities together claiming that they are both promotionally based and share the same basic objective, that of increasing company profits. I am inclined to the latter view, because it is often difficult to view both activities separately when it comes to actual implementation, but more importantly because the projection of the company image and customer relations are marketing, rather than administrative activities. Budget allocation and monitoring are also simplified by considering both key functions under one head.

PR in the sense of both "public" and "press" relations is another way of communicating with a target market by what could be termed more subtle means, ie more subtle than direct display advertising or by using a salesforce. Many organisations are restricted in the wide use of ordinary advertising to promote themselves or their services by virtue of professional ethics (chartered surveyors), or by law (cigarette manufacturers and, no doubt, alcohol companies in the near future). The consumer companies who need to communicate strongly and frequently with a large market and yet face barriers to advertising will switch considerable resources to a wide range of PR activities.

We have seen a great increase in the use of sponsorship as a PR activity, especially of sports events. Many sports events would, in fact, not continue if it were not for the financial support of a varied number of British and overseas consumer companies. Banks seem keen on the idea at present and are sponsoring a number of important sporting events in the United Kingdom and abroad.

I seriously doubt the value of sponsorship as a means of generating new business. I can appreciate the aim of the high-street banks in using sponsorship to create or maintain an image and can see the value of using a particular event to entertain important clients, but I believe that consumer companies, especially those involved in the mass market industries, fool themselves into believing that sponsorship actually produces more sales in the long term. It is more likely to be a case of using surplus advertising appropriation without any real objective in mind.

However attractive the proposition may appear, I do not feel that sponsorship has a role to play in the promotion of a chartered practice, either in terms of the firm itself or in the selling of property. There are two reasons. Firstly, the activity would encourage criticism from the very market to which the practice is trying to sell and, secondly, I cannot imagine clients agreeing to sponsor events in order to aid the disposal of their property.

Having said this, I do recommend, however, that practices should seriously consider participating in events that are being sponsored by somebody else, taking, for example, a hospitality marquee or display unit at a major sporting event. This can be particularly valuable for a residential practice but equally useful to commercial agents *if* participation is properly planned and exploited. Here we do have a problem as virtually all the firms I have seen in this environment are hopelessly inept at selling or projecting the practice to an audience. Surveyors should not feel dismayed, since many consumer companies with trained personnel are unable to get this activity right either. I hope to offer advice in Chapter 9.

The use of the press can be a valuable communicative tool for any commercial undertaking. Research has strongly indicated that editorial matter is read more than technical articles unless there is a specific reader interest, and significantly more than paid-for display advertising. The secret is to ensure that copy matter actually gets printed. This means that items prepared must be newsworthy, simple and of genuine interest to the target audience.

It is important to remember that journalists invariably overestimate their own and their paper's importance and influence. To know and understand press contacts is therefore vital, so that what is prepared is acceptable and will be used in the particular publication selected. The editors of the property press will almost always accept items for publication and often complain that insufficient use is made of their publications by practices who have good stories to tell. National daily newspapers with weekly property inserts, such as the *Financial Times*, are much more selective and will not accept bland uninteresting items from practices that they do not know. I doubt very much that an item in the *Financial Times* aimed at promoting a property or development is as effective as one in *Estates Gazette*, yet an article announcing a successful deal may be better placed with a large national daily in order to promote the practice itself.

The alternative to the practice preparing its own material — and here I totally disagree with Nigel Stephens, who suggests that a trained surveyor is also a good copywriter — is to arrange for a specialist to write articles and supply photographs. Any PR agency of reputation will have copywriters, usually trained journalists on its staff as well as photographers and creative designers.

Often a journalist employed by a particular paper will prepare a feature on, say, industrial and commercial development in the West Midlands and interview the property practices in that area as part of his research. The selection of cities or regions cannot easily be based upon market forces and must be left, therefore, to the journalists or publisher. The more indiscriminate press will often attempt to apply pressure on the local agents, developers and local authorities to take supportive advertising to accompany the feature. One theory is that the target market will focus its attention on the feature because of its special interest.

I have been involved with a number of "special features", both as an advertiser and/or contributor, and have often felt that the random selection of material tends not to fit with one's promotional planning. Some publications, fortunately outside the property press, attempt to exploit the gullibility of the untrained and the inexperienced across a wide range of commercial and government organisations.

A PR agency will undertake to promote a practice or development in every way possible at the least cost. It is important to involve the agency at an early stage and to allow them to participate in the development of a corporate style, literature, site boards, etc, as well as taking care of press and public relations. As with advertising agencies, a PR outfit can be retained on an agreed fee basis and should be invited, with others, to tender for any project. Regular meetings are necessary for monitoring and achievement reviews.

Broad recommendations for the use of public and press relations as a promotional tool by the marketing surveyor or valuer are presented here as a summary:

(a) The value of public and press relations for promotion is in informing a target market about services or premises rather than persuading to seek information.

(b) PR can be cost-effective in establishing or enhancing the reputation of a practice. This will generate new business simply because clients and customers will be attracted to those firms who appear to have a reputation for professionalism and success, even though this may not actually be true.

(c) As with any promotional activity, PR should not be used in isolation but should form part of the promotional plan within the marketing mix. The effectiveness of any PR activity will be greatly reduced if it is not part of an integrated effort.

(d) Sponsorship as a PR activity is expensive. There is little evidence to support the theory that sponsorship generates new business, but for large multi-nationals this activity is seen as a viable means of using profits and of attempting to enhance the company's public reputation. I do not feel that there is a role for sponsorship for the property practice or developer.

(e) Relationships with the property and public press should be cultivated and nurtured. This should be the responsibility of the top management of the practice, working closely with their PR agency or in-house specialists.

(f) Copywriting for the press is as specialised as writing advertising matter and should be left to a specialist who may be a member of the in-house marketing team, a retained consultant, or one of the advertising or PR agency staff. Expecting a surveyor or valuer to write promotional material is equivalent to asking a marketer to prepare a valuation report.

(g) Participate in and support press features on development or property marketing subjects, but use advertising in support of the feature as a PR tool rather than a generator of sales leads.

(h) Invite PR agencies to submit proposals for promoting the practice, new developments or existing premises for which instructions have been received. Each agency should be interviewed following their proposal submission, and, if appointed, be encouraged to contribute to the thinking of the property professionals at an early stage.

8.3. Sales promotion

Sales promotion includes all those activities which communicate with the target market but are not covered by advertising or public and press relations. In consumer markets, sales promotion is regarded as a tactical tool of a short-term nature, designed to stimulate sales. This stimulation comprises mainly incentives which are designed to capture attention and offer some inducement to purchase, generally within a short timescale.

Relating sales promotion to the property world requires a wider overview, as incentives are perhaps inappropriate for stimulating markets. The thought of chartered practices offering sales inducements to, say, property developers, is intriguing but still disallowed by the professional societies.

Before proceeding with the remainder of this chapter, it is worth repeating that in promotional planning for the surveyor we are considering not only the promotion of the practice itself in order to attract new instructions with new clients, but also the promotion of property to attract a buyer. The explanation and discussion of the various activities apply equally to both, only the style of application and levels of expenditure may vary. Space does not permit a detailed examination of the suitability of each activity to the varying objectives of surveyors, practices, developers or government departments. My intention here is to provide a general introduction to the various aspects of promotion.

In discussing the items listed below I have drawn upon two totally different sources of opinion as well as my own experience. This exercise has proved to be extremely interesting, since one source is David Cadman and Leslie Austin-Crowe and their book *Property Development*[6], representing the property experts' view, while the other is *Industrial Advertising and Publicity* by Norman Hart[5], a marketer who has considerable experience in promotion but, to my knowledge, has never been involved in property marketing.

(a) Direct mail (mailshots)

Cadman/Austin-Crowe: Mailshots are seen as "effective and relatively economic". The accurate compilation and updating of mailing lists is felt to be very important as well as the need to ensure that the message is short and sharp. Letters should appear to be original with an original signature.

Hart: Viewed as one of the major channels of persuasion available for "reaching a prospect and achieving maximum impact", direct mail is a versatile tool and a cheap method of communication. It is vital, however, to ensure that the mailing list has been properly compiled, as mailshots to non-prospects are useless. Thus Hart sees the definition of target audiences as extremely important.

Mailshots have been a traditional mainstay of the commercial agent for a long time but I believe that this method is beginning to lose its effect. There is a limit to the number of prospects in the market place at any one time and as more and more industrial and commercial property, both new and existing, comes on to the market so the diminishing target audience is subject to more and more mailshots. Everyone seems to be sending property details to the top 1,000 companies in the United Kingdom and each sender has convinced himself, or his client, that this is sound promotion. I have my doubts. Is it necessary to keep property managers informed of new market entries, or will they simply depend upon the property press? What level of genuine response do agents receive from mailshots?

The real problem may be the difficulty of compiling an appropriate target mailing list as, to my knowledge, no research has ever been undertaken to establish which companies are potential customers, let alone who within the company would be the proper recipient of the mailshot. It is assumed by the agent that the top 1,000 companies are all prime prospects. My criticism of agents' current practice is the lack of effort in establishing the objectives for a mailshot, in attempting to identify target audiences and in follow-up.

To be effective today, mailshots must form part of an integrated campaign, especially where salesmen will be chasing leads via the telephone. Other basic parameters should be adhered to:

    (i) Have objectives been established?
    (ii) Have target audiences been defined and lists compiled?
    (iii) Have targets been set on responses and follow-up?
    (iv) Have all staff been briefed?

As with advertising and editorial matter, writing direct mail copy is a skill not taught to the surveyor or valuer. Outside expertise is required.

(b) Literature

Cadman/Austin-Crowe: Included under "advertising material", literature is seen as expensive to produce and rapidly dated. Nevertheless, it is admitted that "first impressions count and often it is the brochure or leaflet which gives a prospective customer his first impression". When designing literature, it is considered necessary to decide first on subject matter and second on the type of readership.

Hart: The author clearly recognises the differences between prestige "image-building" publications about the company, technical publications and sales literature. Less than 25% of all literature is actually read, which does not mean that cheapness is justified but rather that "more importance centres on what is produced and its quality". To be effective and efficient, literature must be part of the promotional strategy, starting from defined objectives. Instead it is often "ad hoc, unplanned, hurried, ill-conceived and sometimes quite inappropriate". Hart also makes the valid point that many over-estimate the level of understanding that the public has about products and services.

In the property market it is obviously impossible to present the "product" itself, namely premises, directly to a prospective purchaser in his office or plant. It is often also very difficult to persuade the purchaser to travel to view the product himself. Despite the most emphatic denials by experienced practitioners, first impressions are extremely important and the quality, reputation, credibility and professionalism of any agent and/or the property he may be promoting at that time are projected by a piece of visual material.

This is a simple fact and has long been recognised by marketers, especially those who have had responsibilities for "brand management" and packaging. The clever presentation of a mediocre product can produce spectacular sales, particularly in circumstances where a number of similar products exist in a non-price-sensitive market. Buyers are using the same set of emotions in the purchase decision, it is only the scope that varies.

Literature and all other visual material are a means of communicating with a target market and can only be effective by creating the right first impression and by putting over the sales message. Let us consider these two functions.

Commercial agents could gain much by properly presenting themselves and their services to potential buyers. My research has revealed that many firms' brochures vary from nothing at all to boring prose about how long they have been established, number of partners, etc. Others depend upon slipping a few words about their firm into the back of an annual property report.

Much more attention is paid to producing brochures or leaflets for the disposal of premises. Here the standards of good taste and impressive production have often given way to poor imagery and corny creativity. Agents and clients have allowed themselves to be misled by artists and designers, some of whom may even be in-house, into believing that trendy design will sell property. A few examples of the good, the bad and the ugly, as ranked by myself, are shown in Plates 14 to 22.

A surveyor who knows and understands his target market should also know the kind of decision-maker at whom he is aiming his literature. It is this that dictates the design and quality of the brochure, *not* the creative whim of a designer. Briefing is critical and the marketing surveyor must always take this responsibility.

In distinguishing between the functions of literature, Hart is simply stating what is obvious to a marketer but is completely overlooked by many agents. Focused literature has much more impact than that which is generalised. Too much emphasis is placed by commercial agents on the "product" rather than the "consumer". You will recall that in Chapter 1 I wrote about product orientation!

If a development aimed at the high-technology user has been properly researched, designed and built for that industry then the literature must be part of that development and marketing process. The understanding of the market and familiarity with the needs of the high-tech consumer will be clearly reflected in the design and wording of the brochure, while the sales message read by a high-tech company decision-maker will be aimed at *him* not at the world in general. His first impression is enhanced and consolidated by this simple yet very effective strategy. The benefits to the companies in the target market are spelled out and, most importantly, are based on a real knowledge of need obtained during the research phase.

One of the more difficult promotional problems facing a commercial agency at present is in the disposal of existing premises. Most commercial premises, especially shops, can be described in only one or two ways in literature or advertisements. Offices are considered likely to appeal to a limited group of users, but semi-industrial operations such as electronics testing, which will be a big market, should not be ignored as potential office takers. It will not always be the insurance company or accountant that takes office space.

Industrial premises have the widest opportunities of all but rarely do we see literature for existing premises focused on one particular sector. The theory that literature geared to product, rather than the market, will appeal to the widest audience is often the rationale used. This approach fails to exploit any potential that the property may have for particular industrial sectors. It simply becomes another part of the growing stock of "premises suitable for mixed use, strategically located, etc, etc".

The reorientation of literature toward the consumer will open a whole range of new and exciting doors for the marketing surveyor. The practice, too, should reappraise the objectives of its own partnership brochure, if it has one, with a view to spelling out the benefits to potential clients rather than stating what components make up the structure of the firm.

In the past few years the amount of property of all kinds on the market and the valiant attempts of some practices to reach the consumer have resulted in the appearance of property catalogues or magazines produced by individual, or groups of, practices. Quality and style vary considerably, as can be seen from the selection of front covers shown in Plates 23 to 28. The idea seems to have been started by residential practices and has now been taken up by commercial agents, who either produce their own document or join with others to advertise in material produced by newspaper publishers. I consider these journals to be generally good in that they constitute an attempt to target a consumer at least in price or geographical terms. I do not yet see, however, any publications focused on a particular industrial or commercial sector.

(c) Site boards/posters

Cadman/Austin-Crowe: Care should be taken in the positioning of the site board or poster to achieve maximum impact. The advertisement should "convey its message at a glance" and the board should be well maintained and cleaned. A shoddy board casts doubt upon the quality of the development itself.

Hart: Posters represent "a first-class medium for getting across the basic sales message" but location is critical. They can also be effectively used as direct mail pieces.

Experience has shown that this traditional promotional technique is very effective in property letting and yet still receives insufficient attention by the marketing surveyor in respect of:

— design — wording — location
— maintenance — scope

The purpose of a signboard or poster is to project to a consumer a sales message that will benefit him, not to advertise the practice itself. Too much information will not be read, let alone memorised, and how can a potential buyer act upon the information if he cannot remember it? Colour is not used enough, yet a great deal of non-property advertising is now in colour. Regular maintenance is, of course, critical and frequently forgotten. Insufficient use is made of the construction period of a site which affords superb opportunities for creating interest and excitement.

Plates 29 to 36 show typical examples of agents' site boards in both the United Kingdom and United States. There is considerable variation in design and quality, clearly illustrating the points made above. The general approach to site boards by commercial agents is, in my opinion, routine and uninspired, yet it is agreed that first impressions are important and the site board may be a prospective purchaser's first visual contact with a property.

(e) Films and photographs

Cadman/Austin-Crowe: Films are considered to be effective but only for a limited time, as they quickly date. The authors favour a visual presentation using colour slides, since this is much cheaper and more flexible.

Hart: In terms of impact, films are regarded as one of a number of coordinated media "which impress a common message" on a buyer but are thought to have much greater impact than press advertising. Cost dictates that defined objectives and a real understanding of this media are necessary before commitment. "Still photography is the raw material of sales promotion" and other communicative activities: it should not be regarded as being applicable to one subject area only.

The recent introduction of video-tape filming should have made a considerable impact on the promotion of commercial and industrial property, but there appears to be little evidence of this medium of the future being snatched up by the property profession. A video-tape of about 10 minutes' duration can cost between £5,000 and £10,000 when made and edited by a professional firm. This is a small proportion of many advertising budgets, and yet a copy of the video can be sent by post to a prospective purchaser or enquirer, obviating the need for a visit by a salesman at that initial stage. Impact is considerable but this means that a top-quality video must be produced or first impressions will suffer. The innovative opportunity that video films offer the marketing surveyor is enormous; all that is required is promotional flair and commitment.

Still photography is the most cost-effective promotional material for the majority of commercial agents but is so often undertaken cheaply and badly. Many agents are still using black and white photographs, which are then photocopied for particulars, although a whole industry has evolved in the fast and cheap production of colour prints. Surveyors are not trained photographers and colour photographs taken by a professional will add a new dimension to the "first impression" requirements.

(f) Exhibitions

Cadman/Austin-Crowe: Surprisingly, the authors discuss

exhibitions at length after initially considering them to be expensive and time-consuming. It is suggested that only large developments justify a special exhibition and that alternatives such as participating in a local-authority-organised regional exhibition or trade fair may be better. It is recommended that previous audience levels and content are studied when ascertaining the value of an exhibition and that a firm should "take a stand and experiment". Free exchange of experiences with other exhibitors is also seen as useful.

Hart: For many organisations, exhibitions are "often an expression of faith rather than fact", with the budget determined intuitively by a senior manager. Hart claims that there is more money wasted at exhibitions than in any other medium, which is a paradox since the aim is to save money by contacting more buyers in one place and at one time than could possibly be achieved by a field salesman. It is necessary to define the objectives of an exhibition and to build into the event a maximum of efficiency in order to achieve the required result at the least cost.

Hart is absolutely right here. Exhibitions are valuable as part of the promotional mix, never in isolation. The Institute of Directors published a guide in 1969 which contains advice for potential exhibitors, including never trying an exhibition "to see how it goes". The institute also rightly advised that no exhibition, however cheap, should be considered unless it fulfils some clearly-defined marketing objective.

Carefully selected exhibitions can offer considerable opportunities for the marketing orientated practice in terms of impact, image projection, development of contacts, etc. Both the practice and its current portfolio can be promoted and integrated with supportive advertising, and direct mail. This communication medium appears to be effective, since between 1976 and 1980 expenditure on exhibitions in the United Kingdom rose from £79m to £202m — an increase of 156%. Not all surveyors are, however, good salesmen, and proper attention must be paid to staff selection and training for an exhibition as well as to design and supporting literature. Consideration should also be given to including clients and tenants in an exhibition programme.

(g) Other means of promotion

The Cadman/Austin-Crowe team mention a few other promotional activities in their book. They recommend maintaining contact with professional advisers, banks and Chambers of Commerce. This public and professional relations activity is necessary partly to keep a finger on the pulse of the property market and because many service organisations do advise companies on property matters. What one is looking for here, of course, is contacts who will recommend the practice to a company or organisation wishing to purchase or dispose of premises, obtain expert services or evaluate a development proposal. Personal recommendation is a positive generator of business for the marketing surveyor and there is no need, in my opinion, to be embarrassed or cagey about it. Throughout my professional career, I have always recommended to any enquirer the firm that has marketed itself professionally and has bothered to make and maintain contact.

Hart would view this activity as part of the normal work of a salesman and therefore would not include it in a book about industrial publicity. He does, however, devote a chapter to public relations, which was discussed earlier.

The question of "give-aways" as a promotion tool is an interesting recent development where one is trying to strike a balance between cost, impact and good taste. Cadman and Austin-Crowe see the odd ballpoint pen and notepad as having a useful function, while Hart mentions the need for careful consideration on what to give and how and when to give it.

I recommend that each subject area should have its supporting "give-away" material as an effective aid to sales promotion and that the design and quality be geared to the target audience. The subject area will be the practice itself, a development scheme or existing premises upon which instructions have been received. In each case, it is essential that the "brand name" or corporate symbol be clearly shown on the "give-away". Items used may include golf tees, keyrings and pens (suitable for exhibitions), diaries, calendars and notepads (to give to enquirers), through to desk clocks, calculators and other items of office equipment for important clients.

Christmas time can be an excellent opportunity for sales promotion as, apart from wine and Stilton cheese, the sending of the traditional Christmas card continues to be as effective as ever in maintaining good relationships.

Launching ceremonies are felt to be valuable by Cadman and Austin-Crowe as a means of obtaining publicity and local community involvement. I agree, but only if the topping-out or opening ceremony is an integral part of the promotional campaign, so that coordination with advertising or sales visits can be used to maximise effective penetration.

Fitting out part of the development with equipment and furniture for sales promotion is obviously excellent but everything should be maintained in good order for as long as the property has a majority of space unoccupied.

Sales aids are another part of sales promotion, mentioned here in advance of Chapter 9 because the design and use of the salesman's presentation equipment is an important part of promotion. The marketing surveyor has the choice of a wide variety of aids at his disposal when acting as salesman. It should be remembered, too, that the chartered surveyor's or agent's office is also part of the sales promotion of the practice, especially when the practice is undertaking a promotional campaign to generate new business for itself.

8.4. Budgeting

The most difficult question for the surveyor or agency planning a promotional campaign is "how much do we spend?" Investigations made by McGraw Hill in the British engineering industry revealed that 40% of budgets were a fixed figure each year related to overheads, 30% had no known basis and 20% were based on a percentage of the previous year's turnover. My own experiences show that property promotion costs are also derived from inappropriate criteria, which are determined not by the objectives of the promotion strategy but by some arbitrary guess such as what the client feels he can afford. A "10% of costs" rule often applies, but the professional property adviser will find it increasingly difficult to justify any promotional spend to a client in a depressed market situation.

Despite the difficulties of budgeting, I do not entirely accept the view of Cadman and Austin-Crowe, who in their one paragraph on promotional expenditure say: "There are no rules, no infallible methods of calculation to determine the correct amount that should be spent on promotion". An open-ended guess should be unacceptable to any marketing professional and, I would have thought, to a developer or surveyor as well.

An advertising agency will tend to recommend that more advertising with stronger messages is necessary during times of sluggish demand, but the surveyor must resist this pressure by properly developing the promotional plan to ensure that the moneys are spent in the proper place, at the proper time and on the proper message.

One good method for budgeting procedure is termed the "task method" and is based upon a four-stage process:
— Market (What is it? Where is it?)
— Message (For that market)
— Media (Most effective and most direct)
— Measurement (Cost-effectiveness and results)

It is at the media stage that an advertising or PR agency's expertise will be most valuable. The task method requires objectives to be fixed as part of the marketing strategy. This could be to increase "product" awareness by x% or to increase sales in a territory by y%. In property terms the objective may be simply to dispose of a building, to let an entire scheme or to increase awareness of the practice in a new territory. In whatever case the basic thinking process of the task method is a systematic way of attempting to determine a promotional budget.

The "pound contribution method" seeks to relate spend to sales effort by calculating the contribution that promotional revenue makes to total sales. Its benefit is that the marketer can statistically evaluate and compare the contribution to profit of various methods of promotion: for example, new advertising spend can be compared with the alternative of increasing the sales team.

Other methods for setting promotional budgets are based upon a percentage of the previous year's sales or the coming year's forecast and a competitive-parity system which aims to match what competitors are spending. This strikes me as a rather lazy and potentially dangerous practice that can ultimately benefit only the advertising media not the consumer. Some commercial property agents may be guilty of competitive-parity advertising taking, for example, full-colour advertisements in the property press which seem to have the objective of impressing the client rather than promoting the property.

In order to overcome the uncertainty attached to calculating promotion budgets, large consumer companies have developed mathematical models. The parameters used as input to the models include sales records, market shares and consumer response data. Unfortunately, models will not help the marketing surveyor in determining a budget for the promotion of an existing factory or a new office block.

How does a commercial agent determine a promotional budget? Current practice seems to be based on experience and what the client and agent jointly deem to be an appropriate amount, rather than any systematic method. Because this particular marketing function of the agent is not given the correct priority and importance by the practice itself and neither is the promotion based upon any kind of strategy, the budgeting is inevitably haphazard and unplanned. The result can be wasted promotion and increased costs for the client. The ineffectiveness of this kind of campaign may then be explained away as "an indication of the state of the market", or "there was insufficient advertising, more is needed", rather than admitting that the promotion had not been properly planned and budgeted.

8.5. Monitoring and control

Of all the problems associated with promotional planning, the most acute must be control of costs and measuring the effectivenss of a campaign. The formulation of a detailed budget, with each item costed within a timescale, will enable the surveyor to monitor costs. Advertising or PR agencies can be commissioned on a fixed-fee basis and instructed not to exceed agreed cost levels on particular promotional activities without permission.

It is not suggested that every building to be let and every development scheme should have its own full-scale promotional plan. There are obviously situations where this would not be required. It is, however, quite feasible to offer each client a variety of promotional packages ranging from a couple of advertisements to the full-scale integrated campaign. The skill is in offering the right package which the client will see is tailormade for his objectives and can be accommodated within his budget.

The client should be presented with a full-costed plan, which he can comment on or alter as desired, as long as the implications of any alterations are clearly explained by the agent. In order to properly design the promotional plan, the agent must be involved in the development of a scheme, or the decision to let existing premises, at a very early stage so that he can contribute his expertise to the "thinking" of the client or developer. All too often the agent receives instructions after all key decisions have been taken and the promotional budget fixed by the client. Equally, of course, the client often finds himself agreeing to spend considerable resources on an unfocused promotional campaign prepared by the agent.

Campaign evaluation is both difficult and expensive, yet I believe it is inevitable that clients will press more and more for meaningful results from their expenditure, other than just a list of enquiries generated. L S Rodger, in his book *Marketing in a Competitive Economy*[7], compares the non-accountability of promotional costs with running a business without book-keeping.

I believe that it is professionally unacceptable for an agent to propose an advertising campaign with no clearly defined objectives, with little or no information on the target market and the most effective and appropriate communications channel, with copy and design prepared by a trainee surveyor, without any proposals for evaluation, and then to expect his client to pay the bill.

Accountability and a measure of the effectiveness of promotional expenditure is important. There are nearly 20 sources of data based upon desk and field research, as well as sales statistics, for the basic evaluation of an advertising campaign. This level of detailed research enables the surveyor to evaluate each component of a campaign, which, after all, usually constitutes the majority of the promotional budget and demands much attention. The information can be reported to the client before, during and after the campaign. Given the difficulties of the market at present, the property owner or funding institution will then feel that at least an analytical and sales orientated approach is being made to the design and implementation of the promotional plan.

My recommendations for promotional planning are presented here as a check-list, which the marketing surveyor or professional practice can use irrespective of the "product" and which assumes that the firm is now a marketing orientated unit, dedicated to consumer needs, with sufficient marketing expertise in-house, or easily available from outside sources, to both understand and implement the recommendations.

(1) Define the objectives of the promotional campaign and relate these to the overall marketing strategy. (All segmentation and target analyses must have been incorporated.)
(2) Define the proposed "communications mix" for the particular target market and explain reasons for the selection and emphasis.
(3) Show each activity as an integrated campaign on a flowchart with specified time periods.
(4) Cost the proposals and present the entire plan to the client. Modify only if under extreme pressure, as the costs have been based upon the plan and not the budget available.
(5) Establish a budgetary control system.
(6) Design the evaluative and reporting procedures.

Considerable savings can be achieved at an operational level under item (2) without any loss of effectiveness. These can be substantiated by research, and I have mentioned some earlier, for example:

Keep advertisements to a maximum of three press outlets.
Concentrate on editorial and press relations.
Reduce wording on advertisements, to gain maximum impact from available space.
Reduce wording on literature.
Retain advertising or PR agencies on a fee basis.

The property practice would also benefit from a greater concentration on training surveyors in promotional skills or from buying-in expertise to create an in-house team operating under the direct control of the marketing partner.

Chapter 8. References.

[1] "What makes advertising effective?". Herbert Krugman. Harvard Business Review. April 1975.

[2] "The Practice of Estate Agency". Nigel Stephens. The Estates Gazette Limited. 1980.
[3] "What is the real impact of advertising?" Jean-Jacques Lambin. Harvard Business Review. June 1975.
[4] "Advertising Agency Services: make or buy?" Derek Newton. Harvard Business Review. August 1965.
[5] "Industrial Advertising and Publicity". Norman Hart. Associated Business Programmes Ltd. 1978.
[6] "Property Development". David Cadman and Leslie Austin-Crowe. SPON. 1983
[7] "Market in a Competitive Economy". L. S. Rodger.

CHAPTER 9
Selling

At various stages in the previous chapters, references have been made to the selling function and how it relates to the marketing of property. Readers should by now have a clear understanding of the marketing structure of a typical commercial company. The last, and possibly the most important, component in the structure is the salesman. (I use this term in preference to "sales person", which I think is corny, but I am under no illusions with regard to the power and success of "female salesmen". I do not consider property selling to be a male-dominated area.)

The sales activity is part of promotion, being but one of the channels of persuasion referred to earlier. However, it differs from, say advertising, in that the salesman can analyse, evaluate and report on the response from the target market. He can also undertake research to identify opportunities for his company and contribute to the strategic thinking of his top management. What a pity it is that the chartered practices and commercial agents in this country have never realised the potential of a salesman, although to be absolutely fair, many residential agents are actually trying to perform a selling task, albeit in a very passive way.

In my view, current selling practice in the industrial and commercial property world lacks consumer orientation, is unresponsive and unprofessional. While I can understand the lack of appreciation of marketing as a skill owing to lack of training, it is more difficult to explain the non-selling attitude of the average general practice because the professional training of the staff covers "letting" activities at length. Furthermore, many still confuse the term selling with advertising, promotion and marketing.

A glance through the 1976 CALUS report *The Property Development Process*[1] will substantiate what may appear to some to be undue criticism. Despite the fact that the report is seven years old, the contributors represent a good cross-section of the thinking that still seems to pervade the profession. Under "Letting and selling" of offices, the writer claims that the agent "is the expert in marketing and in letting and selling" — a real mix of terms and a surprising claim when one considers the RICS training programme and examination syllabus at that time. Having drawn an analogy between Beechams and Rolls-Royce, whom he claims are market-orientated and sales-orientated respectively, the writer then states that "letting and selling agents have to be both sales and marketing orientated" — a view that I agree with but not as separate, somehow unrelated, activities as suggested.

The chapter on letting shops in the CALUS report does not mention marketing or selling at all but describes at length the procedure for appointing "letting agents". Believing that buying shops is different from buying industrial premises, and discounting advertising as a viable means of "publicity", the writer clearly advocates a direct selling approach to potential buyers without once mentioning the term "selling".

A glimmer of hope, however, comes from the chapter on "selling and letting" of industrial premises where, under the sub-heading of "Marketing", the author launches into a description of the usual traditional promotional activities. He does, however, advocate the appointment of a public relations firm, thus recognising that surveyors are not PR experts, but warns that the agent must stay in control to ensure "that the property is not marketed just like any other commodity such as a new brand of washing machine powder". This is sound advice, and more follows a few pages later when, unlike the other writers, this surveyor actually covers the selling function, albeit under another term — "negotiator". He also recommends that practices should place greater emphasis upon "better selling techniques", including training of their agency staff.

Cadman and Austin-Crowe[2], acting as developers, beg the question "Why appoint agents?" when considering the advantages and disadvantages of an in-house selling team — a question that many like the newly formed Barratts Commercial would have little difficulty in answering. The authors take a charitable line, however, and having stated that the estate agent is traditionally responsible for selling, they give six reasons for this:

(a) Agents are often in a better location for attracting business (by virtue of having city-centre offices).
(b) A good agent should have detailed knowledge of the particular market in which he operates.
(c) A national agent normally has a greater understanding of the larger and more complex schemes and has more direct and more frequent contacts with the larger companies.

(d) A local agent normally has a better understanding of the local market.

(e) Agents bring to the project additional knowledge and experience.

(f) They provide selling expertise.

Note that the selling expertise of the agent is included, but how limited the list is in view of the potential that could be offered by a marketing-orientated practice!

If selling, or letting and negotiating, is considered to be such an integral part of the agent's services and a vital skill of the surveyor, why is it still done so badly? Several answers are offered for consideration.

Surveyors are not trained in the art of selling and often have the wrong personality in the first place. Let us not confuse negotiating, after the selling decision has been made, with selling. Most established practices are not consumer orientated and have a senior partner structure which is outdated, too conservative and probably anti-agency. They consider that "salesmen" are a necessary evil and that marketing is just another term for advertising. Little has been done by the profession to dispel this myth.

Many practices are not committed to the selling function, even in times of economic stress. Evidence of this is apparent in such things as the design and layout of offices, the way the telephone is answered and the lack of concern by staff for the customer. Despite commission schemes as an incentive, too many staff are untrained, passive, lack self-motivation and are hopeless at pursuing sales leads. They also lack the ability to identify opportunities for the practice. Despite actually operating a "hard-sell" system, many agents hide behind a veil of professional snobbery, claiming that the best results are achieved through a "soft-sell" approach, a method that they neither understand nor actually operate. As J E Rushton of Edward Rushton Son & Kenyon once said: "The profession should be so much better equipped to deal with the likely increasing pressure on agency firms to produce the goods in the cut and thrust of the property market."

9.1. What is selling?

The fact that the property profession considers that the art of selling, as part of a surveyor's or valuer's expertise, is obtained and somehow developed by instinct, is almost beyond belief. The difference between a professional salesman and a professional who thinks he can sell is considerable and the whole area of selling and sales management itself is vast. In this chapter I can only skim the surface, trying to relate modern selling skills to the property profession.

"Selling is the most dynamic force of marketing because it is the only activity that generates revenue." This definition by John Stapleton[3] fits the commercial agency, whether applied to the selling of expert services or to the selling of property. Readers who recall the definition of marketing will realise that here the discussion is about "satisfying consumer requirements" and that marketing is not another word for selling.

The best salesmen are those that realise that people buy products that are going to benefit them, not for any other reason. So it is with companies or organisations, except that in these buying circumstances the salesman has to persuade a group or "buying committee" that they will collectively benefit from buying his product. The choice between product A and product B, where benefits appear to the group to be equal, will often depend upon the personality and professionalism of the salesman.

"Sales" staff in a commercial agency are often faced with selling a property to a buying group, such as a company board. This is much more difficult than selling a consumer product to a housewife and emphasises the need for a proper approach to the appointment, training and management of the agency salesmen. It also opens up another area where opinions among selling professionals differ. What kind of person should be appointed as a salesman? In his article "How to buy and sell professional services", Warren Wittreich[4] describes two basic types of salesman in the service sector: one is "the professional salesman [who] sees his major personal strength as that of being able to sell" and depends upon others for expert technical input when required, while the other type is "the professional who can also sell". The latter sees himself as a technical expert and a qualified professional *but* can also demonstrate his own and his firm's capabilities when required. Wittreich claims that the service firms "represented by true professionals are far more valuable to their clients than those represented by professional salesmen". This would seem to substantiate the view held by most surveyors and valuers but not, I suspect, by non-chartered commercial and industrial agents.

Wittreich qualifies his view by indicating that the true professional is characterised by two important things: firstly, his ability to demonstrate his knowledge and skill in a particular area and, secondly, to recognise his limits in both. The lack of commitment to marketing research by the professional practice already severely limits knowledge.

Nigel Stephens[5] admits in his book that it was not his intention to cover "selling" in detail, but he does discuss the personal characteristics found from American experience to be the most important for a good salesman. Unlike myself, he wisely does not stray into the area of professional salesmen or selling professionals but agrees that good ones are "born and not made". His view of current selling practice, however, is quite clear and I fully support it: "It is not sufficient in the estate agency context for managers or negotiators to accept the present level of achievement."

I do not agree with the views held by Wittreich which suggest that a qualified professional can turn to selling as and when required as if it were a casual activity. The professional quickly finds himself in trouble during times of economic hardship when other professionals, who have taken selling seriously, compete in the offering of expert advisory services. In selling premises, it is the professional who can discuss the structural attributes of a building with a production director but finds himself completely outclassed by an effective promotional campaign involving the professional salesmanship of an enlightened and aggressive competitor.

The answer must surely be to build a sales team comprising different strengths, so that the kind of salesman recruited into the team depends upon the job he has to do, the product and service he has to sell and the types and levels of buyer involved. Cyril Hudson, in *The Making of a Modern Salesman*[6], recommends a balanced structure for an industrial sales team, made up of technically or professionally qualified salesmen who can either sell well or can be trained to sell well. They should be capable of selling services or products to top management, where knowledge is vital to success, and they should also be able "to negotiate well at executive levels through a capacity to create a parity of personal esteem". These salesmen would be supported by less technically qualified men, whose main strength is to sell well and who are capable of involving technical staff when necessary to meet the growing expertise of the buyer or buying group.

9.2. Implications for the commercial practice

It would seem that the requirement to sell both the expert services of a practice and clients' property would best be served by a sales structure along the lines described above. Many practices do have this structure, some tend to recruit more surveyors and valuers, and there are others who do not see the value of professionally qualified staff for their particular selling activity.

All practices need to review their sales structure both now and at regular intervals in the future, for as markets change so does the effectiveness of all persuasive channels. Like it or not, everyone in the practice is involved in the selling function, whether they are selling management or valuation services to property owners or a shopping complex to a multi-national retailer. *It is all selling* and the senior partners have the responsibility of ensuring that all levels of staff are committed, including themselves.

It is useful at this point to consider the kind of selling that the commercial agent is involved in, as this can influence the age and experience of the persons in the sales structure. Research undertaken in 1969 by Derek Newton, a lecturer on business administration at the Harvard Business School, sought to relate age and experience to four distinct kinds of selling. These were:

(1) Trade selling — primarily concerned with selling to customers through a wholesaler, retailer or manufacturer.
(2) Missionary selling — to product specifiers such as doctors.
(3) Technical selling — to industrial buyers.
(4) New-business selling — obtaining new accounts and/or new clients.

The last two represent the kind of selling that faces a property practice, in that a form of "technical selling", or problem solving, is inherent in letting premises to companies and "new business selling" is important in obtaining new instructions and new clients.

According to Derek Newton, technical selling is best undertaken by professionally qualified staff in their late twenties or early thirties, and close supervision by top management is essential. This high-performance activity is akin to consulting, as "the ability to identify, analyse and solve customers' problems is vitally important". New-business selling requires a "cold-calling" capability and is best suited to mature, experienced practitioners in their late thirties or forties. These salesmen are rare and independent. Not suited to close supervision, they succeed where younger technical staff do not. Turnover is high and the capability of a new-business seller needs to be recognised by the company in the remuneration paid.

The implications of this research hold no real surprises in that the agency side of the work would seem to be suited to younger surveyors and valuers, leaving the task of obtaining new business to experienced people, a role that may suit the partners of the practice.

Another issue, which seems to be thrown around when discussing property selling, is the "hard-sell/soft-sell" argument. Apparently a lot of property people consider that selling used cars is a "hard-sell" activity and that the "soft-sell" is somehow more professional and dignified. Others definitely use it as an excuse not to sell at all! Nigel Stephens confesses to not having found a definition of "hard-sell" at all and assumes it to mean "aggressive, forceful and pushing".

Drawing upon American and Australian experience as well as his own, he concludes that the "soft-sell" is more applicable to estate agency. Interestingly, he also comments on the fact that in other countries those who sell property are called "salesmen", whereas in the UK they are termed "negotiators".

Cyril Hudson clearly sees the role of the dynamic salesman as the "operational spearhead of the company's marketing targets", a person who will be under increasing pressure to provide information, interpretation, advice and expert services. He believes that personal salesmanship will assume a new dignity in accord with "its ambassadorial, consultancy and advisory status". To achieve this it must discard the "hard-sell" image and any approach to gain business by "guile and flannel". It should also avoid the stereotyped presentation, both verbally and visually (all those repetitive property brochures!) and question the value of that old favourite AIDA (attention, interest, desire, action) as a formula for selling.

This does not mean that the adoption of a "soft-sell" approach is both justifiable and productive for the property practice. In fact, it could be argued that the commercial agent does use a "hard-sell" approach in that a property or scheme is invariably built without any real analysis of market demand, rentals are determined by construction costs rather than market forces and the agent appointed to "procure" tenants. The agent's response to an enquirer is aided by a brochure and can involve a face-to-face discussion where prices are freely quoted, while the customer may have already partly committed himself to buy by virtue of his enquiry. Such activity could hardly be called "soft-sell". In fact, neither term is applicable for today's property professionals where the demands of new technology and international business require a different approach.

The key to creating a successful commercial practice is, I believe, to concentrate on what Philip Kotler calls converting "order-takers" to "order-getters". A normal agency spends a great deal of time processing "orders", where customers are aware of their own needs, probably cannot be influenced and respond to salesmen who are courteous and apparently helpful. This passive-responsive operation is typical of residential agency branch offices that have catalogues of "products" administered by clerical staff. In times of boom, such operations perform reasonably well but have little to do with selling. In times of recession, the system falters, as the staff have become "order-takers" and are incapable of change.

In order to become an "order-getter", which must be the ambition of every surveyor or valuer in general commercial practice, there are two choices of training and development. The first is to become a high-pressure salesman who concentrates on overstating the merits of the property or scheme, criticises other agents, and attempts to give a slick stereotyped presentation. The second choice is to become a problem-solver, the salesman who, as Kotler says, "studies the customer's needs and wants and proposes profitable solutions". This concern for the consumer is effective and presents an image of a salesman that is much more compatible with the marketing concept than the "hard-seller" or "order-taker". Most property professionals would like to consider themselves to be "problem-solvers" but is this true?

Cyril Hudson believes that the new salesman must be positive, creative, persuasive and have a business-winning capacity. All sales staff will be increasingly involved in market research, product development and pricing, becoming the "managers of change that takes place daily in the fluctuating market environment".

9.3. The salesman

Any enlightened agency or practice that is building a new sales team has to consider the sort of person it needs — ideally someone who is both technically qualified and capable of undertaking a problem-solving sales role.

Appearances are extremely important, as personal credibility can be enhanced or destroyed by standards of dress, cleanliness and the kind of car that the salesman uses. Problem-solving depends to a large extent on mutual trust as well as technical understanding and credibility is a cornerstone of trust. Age and professional achievement have been discussed earlier, and the structure of the team will depend upon the tasks it has to perform.

Personality is obviously important and it is worth considering the simplified analysis of personalities as described by Peter Cripps, a sales training consultant. There are four kinds of personality in the buying/selling environment: cold-submissive, cold-dominant, warm-submissive and warm-dominant. It can be seen that the meeting of the wrong types, such as a cold-submissive seller and a cold-dominant buyer will be a disaster from which no sale will result. Equally, although it may seem ideal to have only warm-dominant salesmen in the team, this type of personality finds it difficult to deal with cold-dominant buyers, and so on. The real answer, as Peter Cripps says, is to recruit salesmen who are "capable of diagnosing the buyer type and changing their own personality accordingly".

John Stapleton substantiates this view by describing the successful salesman as a person who, by employing a "sixth sense", can identify and satisfy the customer's unspoken needs and wants. Such salesmen tend to come "from the highly-perceptive members of the community, those that feel mood, sense attitude and respond accordingly. By so reacting they sell themselves to prospects".

A property salesman will be expected to undertake several other tasks in the 1980s in addition to selling:
- (a) *Prospecting* — the agency or practice will spend a lot of money on generating leads for the salesteam by advertising, direct mail etc, but all salesmen will also be expected to search for additional prospects.
- (b) *Communicating* — the art of communicating information to both existing and potential customers about the agency and its services and "products".
- (c) *Servicing* — "after-sales" activities including problem-solving and technical assistance. Existing customers are the agents' best ambassadors, if properly cultivated.
- (d) *Information gathering* — the market research role played by salesmen.

The selling function itself is, of course, not just a matter of sending a brochure to an enquirer and waiting for a response; this is "order-taking". The professional surveyor or valuer who is to be trained to sell must concentrate efforts on a series of steps now regarded as being standard for most sales training programmes. I have adapted the procedure for the property profession:

1. Identification of prospects

This involves the development of sales leads through a range of activities that the surveyor is quite capable of undertaking — regular meetings with retained clients and existing tenants, cultivating sources of referral such as banks or solicitors, joining local business organisations and scanning printed sources of information for clues.

"Cold calling" is still regarded by the RICS and ISVA as canvassing and is considered unethical. It is also viewed by many practitioners as a "hard sell" and therefore an undesirable approach. This is, in my opinion, nonsense and must inhibit a positive approach to the job of selling. As a property owner I would never consider placing instructions with a commercial practice that used only advertising, mailshots and the Chamber of Commerce lunch to generate sales leads.

"Cold calling" or trying to sell to a complete stranger by telephone or face-to-face does, however, require a certain kind of personality. A salesman has two basic fears — of failure in doing the selling job and of rebuff in personal relationships. For the surveyor there may be a third: the basic unwillingness to sell based upon preconceived ideas of professional status and self-image.

Irrespective of the excuses that are put forward by the surveyor for not undertaking a level of "cold calling", today's market situation dictates that a level of this particular style of selling is necessary and proper sales training and enlightened management will help to make the task more enjoyable and effective. Surveyors and valuers are not trained salesmen and even when an aggressive selling stance is adopted by the firm, training is necessary for what are mistakenly believed to be simple selling tasks.

2. Preapproach

Careful preparation prior to a meeting with a prospective buyer can make the difference between a sale and a disaster. The surveyor must be familiar with the company, its products, size, track record, etc, as well as being aware of the size and composition of the "buying group". This will help him to make decisions on the best method of approach as well as the objectives and timing of the visit.

3. Approach

This step entails the surveyor knowing how to meet the prospect in a way that will get the relationship off on the right footing from the start. Because personality and credibility are such important considerations at this stage, the appearance, manner and status of the seller are critical. The style of opening remarks and the careful attention paid to the prospective buyer can make a significant difference.

4. Presentation

The nature of the "product" dictates that in most circumstances the surveyor has to depend upon sales aids for presentation purposes. This is true for the selling of expert services, which are intangible, and also for property, which may be several hundred miles away from the prospect at the time of the sales presentation. The aim of the presentation is to focus on the needs and wants of the buyer and to attempt to satisfy these by using the product benefits to demonstrate to him that he can save or make money. Literature, audio-visual and, in the case of a site visit, the actual "product" itself are all supportive to this aim.

Rosann Spiro and William Perrealt[7] identified the following five influencing strategies that are used by salesmen during a presentation:

(a) Legitimacy — convincing the buyer of the reputation of the practice.
(b) Expertise — demonstrating the knowledge of the buyer's situation as well as his own expertise.
(c) Referant power — an attempt to build on shared characteristics, interests and acquaintances.
(d) Ingratiation — personal favours or offers to the buyer, such as lunch, paid-for site visit and give-aways.

(e) Impression — manipulating impressions of self in order to elicit a more favourable response (referred to above under "personality changes").

5. Handling objections

This involves negotiating, an area in which the surveyor should be a skilled practitioner. Buyers will always pose objections during a presentation, for physchological rather than logical reasons. The book *Selling — The Personal Force in Marketing*, by Crissy and Cunningham[8], discusses nine psychological sales resistances which should be familiar to any property salesman:

(a) Resistance to interference.
(b) Preference for established habits (resistance to a new geographical location).
(c) Apathy.
(d) Reluctance to give up something.
(e) Unpleasant associations with salesmen and/or other persons.
(f) Tendency to resist "domination" (by the salesman).
(g) Predetermined idea (which may not be needs and wants).
(h) Dislike of making decisions.
(i) Neurotic attitude toward money.

A surveyor has to maintain a positive attitude and seek to turn objections into reasons for buying by questioning the prospect and unearthing the underlying problems behind objections. The problem-solving role is obvious here. Sales negotiation forms part of the training of a surveyor so we need dwell no further on this.

6. Closing the sale

The nature of the property sale makes it difficult for the surveyor to adopt conventional techniques in closing. The often protracted negotiations with a buying group, frequently involving a third party, require a different procedure to that of simply obtaining an order at a sales presentation. Nevertheless, training surveyors to recognise and diagnose "closing signals" would give them an edge over "order-takers". The surveyor will find himself attempting to close a sales at a distance, maybe after the person to whom he has made a presentation has discussed the proposal with colleagues in private. Greater attempts should be made to present the proposition to other members of the "buying group", thus winning confidence and agreement on a one-to-one basis. Special presentational literature could also be prepared as supportive data in situations where one member of the "buying group" has to report back to colleagues. The offering of inducements should not be overlooked, a recent example is shown below.

1 DEAL = 4 WHEELS

A brand new MG Mini Metro will be yours if you acquire this building.

Ingram House in John Adam Street, London WC2 is a superbly refurbished self contained office building of 15,800 sq.ft. in a highly accessible location in central London.

For further details on the property...and the car – contact our agents Douglas Young & Company.

DOUGLAS YOUNG & COMPANY
1 Vintners Place
London EC4V 3AD
01-248 3884

LCW LONDON CITY & WESTCLIFF PROPERTIES LTD
PO Box 55
11-13 Holborn Viaduct
London EC1P 1EL 01-236 6241

Closing a sale of expert services should be easier than with property, although the potential buyer will often want time to consider and to discuss the proposition with colleagues. Under these circumstances step no 7 becomes extremely important.

7. Follow-up

For the property professional, I consider effective follow-up to be the most fundamental activity in obtaining new business and closing sales. Yet it appears to be the one area in which the profession consistently fails. No excuses are plausible enough to justify an agency sales team's inability to actively pursue enquiries and leads: it is the key to success in selling.

All buyers need constant reminding of a product's attributes and respond well to a warm, consistent and persuasive attendance by a salesman. More powerful even than this is a genuine and personal concern for the buyer and his needs and wants. It is a fact that the property purchase decision-time can be as long as two years, and it will take a great deal of effort to maintain contact during this period. But what an opportunity to cultivate a personal relationship! The length of decision time is ideal for the problem-solving surveyor, who can actually become so involved with the company and its buying group that he could eventually find himself as a retained adviser.

This "developmental" approach to property selling does not seem to happen in this country. Our traditional passive approach requires only that a brochure is sent in response to an enquiry and if the company is interested it will make contact for further details. Little attempt is made to actively follow up and to become involved with the enquirer and his business so that the problem-solving technique can be effectively exploited.

Follow-up requires proper personal organisation by the salesman, using a positive and innovative attitude. He must care about his prospects and constantly seek ways and means to maintain close contact. A monthly telephone call, Christmas card, personal letters announcing new developments or new services within the practice, visits while "in the area", invitations to launch ceremonies and so on can all be used to good effect.

9.4. Sales management

As Philip Kotler quite rightly says, the major requirements for building a first-class sales force are "attracting good people, motivating them and keeping them". A key factor in this concept is the salary arrangement. Diagram 15 shows performance levels for different pay structures which are:

    (a) Salary only

Figure 15 Sales force performance under different remuneration packages

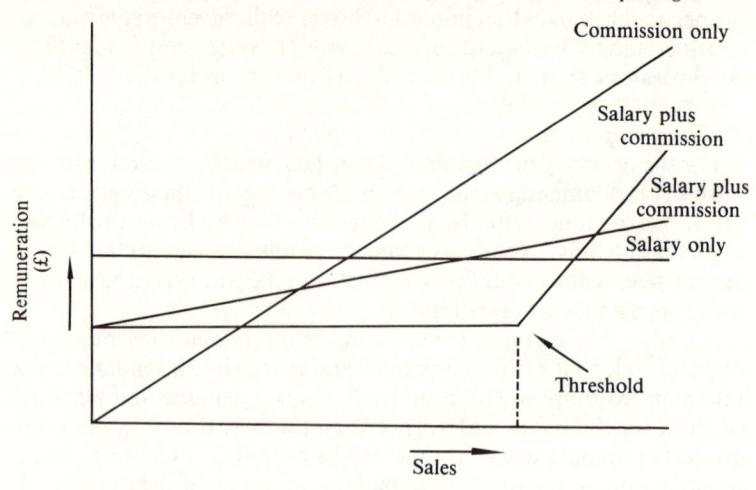

[Graph: Remuneration (£) vs Sales, showing four lines — Commission only, Salary plus commission, Salary plus commission (with threshold), Salary only; Threshold marked on x-axis]

   (b) Commission only
   (c) Salary plus commission
   (d) Salary plus commission at a sales threshold.

Each system has advantages and disadvantages and the choice for management will depend on products and market objectives. It is obvious that each system, except commission only, will appeal to the more mature and conservative person, whereas younger aggressive salesmen will favour a system that relates income directly to effort. However, most salesmen of all ages and experience have certain basic requirements from any job — income regularity, security, reward for above-average performance and fairness. This has tended to give rise to a "salary plus commission" scheme being adopted by most companies and, indeed, property practices. A combination of three elements has been found to be the most satisfactory within this pay system — a fixed amount, irrespective of sales achieved, the commission or bonus for performance at or above a predetermined level, and expenses and fringe benefits, such as pensions, life insurance etc.

Motivation comes not only from the incentive of commission but also from two other sources. Fringe benefits can be both cost-effective and powerful in the motivation of salesmen. Consider the company that pays for an annual holiday for its salesmen and their families, perhaps tying the trip into a national or international sales conference. Then the quality company car, free petrol, Christmas hamper, private hospital scheme and so on can all be used as additional benefits to attract and motivate a salesteam. These need not be confused with schemes to motivate by competition, such as the once-popular "league table" system operated by many consumer companies. The professionally qualified problem-solving surveyor salesman required for today's property practice may not fit in well to a competitive scheme.

The second major motivator for the professional who can sell is good management. All salesmen need to be loved and this means the adoption and implementation of a caring and enthusiastic attitude by the top management. The salesmen are the most important people in the practice and as such demand the respect and support of all other personnel, but especially the senior managers. A partner who does not agree with this philosophy should be removed, as he cannot be contributing to the firm's overall growth and profit objectives.

Staff involved in the selling of a practice's expert services, however, do not fit easily into a commission scheme, which is invariably based on property sales. Here a basic salary plus expenses and fringe benefits will be effective, with a bonus or share of profits paid annually to the top "order-getters".

In all the pay schemes discussed, it is important for the property practitioner to remember that the surveyor/salesman will be undertaking other tasks as well as straight selling; prospecting, researching and communicating are all key functions and should not be given any lesser priority in terms of remuneration.

Another main function of management — and in itself a motivator — is training. John Stapleton[3] says: "Salesmen spend most of their time without direct supervision. They are continuously going through the same routine, numerous times each day, of presenting their products and emphasising and re-emphasising the benefits of particular products. In return, they hear every day all the reasons why most prospects do not buy from their company. Under such constant pressure it is not surprising that an individual salesman becomes disorientated". In other words, they become "stale", apathy then steps in and the sales force have become "order-takers".

Regular sales meetings and training sessions are easy to organise and very beneficial to both the salesmen and the sales manager, or partner with the management responsibility. There are six basic subject areas that should be covered in a property practice's sales training programme:

(1) *The practice* — history, organisation, procedures and objectives.

(2) *The market* — segmentation and analysis reports, sizes, shares, new opportunities and development strategies, problems of buyers.

(3) *The products* — services, properties, schemes, clients and future developments.
(4) *Promotion* — promotional plans, timescales, budgets.
(5) *Sales techniques* — methodology, approach, organisation, presentations, objectives, development of personal skills.
(6) *Support* — the services provided by the sales office, clerical staff and top management.

The further development of personal selling skills requires the involvement of a specialist consultant, who should also be able to advise on most of the other subject areas as well. A marketing-orientated practice, however, should have sufficient expertise in-house to cover most of the organisational and support aspects.

As far as I know, no commercial agencies or chartered practices in the UK organise sales-training programmes for their staff — a sad and unnecessary state of affairs. I have read only two enlightened experts on this matter to date. J E Rushton, in describing the contents of a selling course advertised in 1974 says: "I do not think it will be very long before attendance at these courses will be considered to be part of the training of agency staff." Yet by 1981 Nigel Stephens, writing about motivation, observes: "I know of very few firms who have set out to provide considered, planned and regular training for their sales team and negotiators, and yet it is they who would directly receive the benefit from doing so". How are we going to progress over the next seven years?

9.5. The sales office

In 1981 the cost of a sales "call" in this country was £80 and the cost of sales effort for each purchase about £400. It is inevitable that cheaper forms of communication between seller and buyer will be used to maximise a salesman's time: the telephone is an obvious method and telephone selling is on the increase in this country. In fact, there are a half dozen companies currently offering telephone selling and research services across a wide range of product areas. There are also courses organised by the Institute of Marketing on telephone technique for clerical staff and telephone selling for salesmen, any of which I would recommend from personal experience. The use of the telephone is but one area in which sales support staff are heavily involved and there is much room for improvement in the way in which telephone calls are both received and made.

A firm's image and its professional credibility are also projected by the design of the reception area and offices. I have visited many offices in the past 20 years and can judge the quality and professionalism of the firm, and often its top management, by the "front-office".

Most surveyors are not interior designers and it makes sense to commission a specialist who can properly build into a concept the desired company image. The design must also cater for people, so due attention should be paid to personal facilities and comfort. The "low seats and counter" idea is both negative and unfriendly; and why is it that receptionists, who are of course "sales" staff, never have the facility to serve refreshment to a visitor?

A great number of visitors to a commercial agency must, by definition, be potential buyers and should be made to feel that they are the most important person at that time to everybody in the practice but especially to those in the reception area and sales office. Any property man who has visited a top advertising agency will fully understand what I mean.

Nigel Stephens' book offers very sound advice on the layout of the reception office and, more importantly, the training of the receptionist in a residential agency. Much of what is recommended goes for the commercial agency as well, and I particularly agree that the opening remark to a visitor should be "How can I help you?" instead of the usual rhetoric that one has come to expect from untrained staff.

I was pleased to see the advertisement for Jackson Property Services in *Estates Gazette* in January 1983 for two reasons, firstly because of a statement by the managing director, Alan Robinson. In accounting for their undoubted success in selling houses, he says: "Our in-house training programme taken by all our sales staff emphasises the need to provide the best possible service to the public." Training, then, appears to be part of Jackson's activities. Alan Robinson continues: "We are in a service industry but unfortunately many estate agents don't appear to understand what the word 'service' means".

The second point that pleased me was their attitude towards the sales office and its design. Recognising that image is important and that a careful design provides an opportunity for informative rather than persuasive advertising, Jacksons commissioned a specialist firm of consultants to design their offices in accord with the firm's corporate style. There are dangers, of course, in that design must not be allowed to become an ego-trip for the senior partners; emphasis should be on design for customers and not the firm. Another problem is one that has been mentioned to me on more than one occasion — customers' unfortunate tendency to relate what may appear to be lavish expenditure on offices and reception areas to the fees charged for services. It would be interesting to receive views on this from Jacksons.

A relative newcomer to the commercial agent's office is the computer. Like other service industries, the property practice has been traditionally slow to take advantage of electronics as a time-saver and efficiency maker. I am not suggesting that a computer is a vital piece of equipment and that practices who do not invest soon will lose business as a result. On the contrary, no equipment should be purchased unless it has a definite role to play and can make a positive contribution to long-term cost savings. A great deal of mystique and nonsense surrounds computers, but the advent of the home enthusiast and computer education in schools is doing much to dispel this. For the uninitiated, there are three basic computer systems:

Main frame — enormous-capacity machines requiring temperature- and air-controlled environments and mainly used by large companies, government departments and computer processing bureaus. Typical makes are IBM, ICL and Honeywell and they cost from £250,000 upwards.

Mini — lesser-capacity equipment, still requiring special environments. Nowadays little difference is apparent between main-frame and mini-computers. Makes are ICL, Honeywell, Dek, Digital and many others. Costs are £50,000 to £250,000.

Micros — portable, desk-top computers that started as a home hobbyist product in the USA. Requiring no special facilities and with amazing capacity, these machines are made by over 200 firms, such as Apple, Commodore, Dragon, Sinclair, Televideo, Motorola, Sirius, Torch and Olivetti. (IBM and others have recently broken into this enormous market). Costs for a business system range from £2,000 to £20,000.

The micro-computer system would typically have a visual display unit (VDU) and a keyboard that is basically the same as a typewriter keyboard, making it acceptable to secretarial staff. The VDU may have facilities built in to accommodate the computer disks called "floppy" disks or diskettes, and a printer would be included to provide hard copy. A word-processor is a computer program, not a kind of computer and all micro systems will provide full word processing facilities, ideal for the focused mailshot. Programs can be purchased on a floppy disk. Speeds of operation vary between systems and care should be taken in selecting a machine that will fulfil the major requirement of the firm. A direct-mail facility may call for a different system than a requirement for data storage and retrieval.

An alternative approach to direct mail, other than the use of a word-processing program in-house, is to use a mailing company.

Richard Ellis and Leighton Goldhill both use a firm called Market Location, which claims to be able to identify the right target for a mailshot and to deal with compilation of addresses and despatch of letters. Apart from the danger of confusing target marketing with compiling an address list, I was struck by the remark made by Charles Osborne of Leighton Goldhill in a recent advertisement for the firm: "Market Location is the obvious choice when the alternative is often time-consuming and inefficient personal canvassing you have to do yourself". In no way should the use of an updated mailing list be a substitute for personal selling. Mailshots are strictly a sales-support activity in that they are a means of generating sales leads and do not constitute the total selling effort.

Another word of warning — virtually all computer consultants are retained by manufacturers and will be biased in their advice. A few real consultants do exist, such as Mercator Computer Systems in Bristol, and advice can often be sought from educational establishments, except that these sometimes lack real commercial experience. The National Association of Estate Agents is about to recommend to its members one computer system that can undertake a series of tasks including: property management, property and applicant registers, mailing routines, word processing, valuations and mortgage calculations.

A further basic requirement is the capability of the system to form part of a network linking offices within a group, such as Allen & Harris have in Oxford, or linking firms in a consortium, such as the Property Agents Computer Team (PACT). The aim here is to provide a better "matching" service to customers, although customer-orientation would contradict Allen & Harris's claim that "the computer now dictates where we site our offices because it provides a logical analysis of our territories", which appeared in the July 1983 issue of *Microscope*, a computer newspaper.

While accepting that a computer is an electronic aid to marketing decisions, I really cannot agree with the view expressed in *Microscope* at the beginning of the article on estate agents and micro-computers: "Estate Agents can't claim to be the most honest of people. This bad reputation is recognised and deplored by the more concientious members of the industry and a lot of hope is pinned on computerisation and the resultant wind of change to clear away the bad apples". (Is this a pun?) This kind of nonsense is a slur on the profession and an indication of how naive the writer is in believing, or attempting to persuade the reader to believe, that computerisation is going to change professional standards. The author is also badly informed, as the entire article does not mention the RICS or ISVA or make any reference to the investigations into computers that both bodies have undertaken. Those commercial agents who feel that they may be left behind need not worry, since only 1% of residential agency practices currently have microcomputer systems, according to the article.

What then can the surveyor/salesmen expect in the future by way of electronic aids? Much talk abounds at the moment about the "automated office", with electronic temporary memory typewriters, telecom devices, etc, but for most property practices with a normal budget there is a limit to how much equipment can be purchased. Nothing should be purchased, in my view, that does not fulfil a proper objective aimed at improving customer service or sales efficiency. Whatever equipment it may have, the sales office is the vehicle of communications and contributes significantly to the making of a real team. As Cyril Hudson says: "It means that there can be no gaps of understanding between sales office and salesmen about planning, calling, business seeking, business promotion and overall operational effort."

Chapter 9. References

[1] "The Property Development Process". Centre for Advanced Land Use Studies. 1976.
[2] "Property Development". David Cadman and Leslie Austin-Crowe. SPON. 1983.
[3] "Marketing". John Stapleton. Hodder & Stoughton Paperbacks. 1979.
[4] "How to buy and sell professional services". Warren Wittreich. Harvard Business Review. April 1966.
[5] "The Practice of Estate Agency". Nigel Stephens. The Estates Gazette Ltd. 1980.
[6] "The Making of a Modern Salesman". Cyril Hudson. Crosby Lockwood 1973.
[7] Rosann Spiro and William Pereault. Unpublished paper. University of North Carolina. 1976.
[8] "Selling — The Personal Force in Marketing". W. J. E. Crissy, W. H. and I.C.M. Cunningham. John Wiley & Sons. New York. 1977.

CHAPTER 10
Summary and Conclusions

This chapter will cover three areas aimed at pulling together some broad conclusions. Salient points from the previous nine chapters will provide an executive summary for the marketing partner of the practice and this will be followed by a discussion of recent developments in property marketing that are of considerable relevance. Finally, a glimpse at the future will be attempted, with evidence to substantiate any claim that marketing can and will revolutionise the industrial and commercial property profession

Summary

A main assumption made during the planning of this book was that the target readership wanted to expand and grow either at a personal level or as part of a professional practice. Those not interested in continuing professional or profitable development will obtain little from what has been written. As a marketer, not a surveyor, I have openly and honestly attempted to bring marketing to a profession that has the skills and resources to exploit the philosophy to its advantage.

Chapter 1 covers the background to marketing and its development in the United Kingdom. Although the discipline has been around for a long time, the need was never greater than now for a better understanding of the consumer of property and his needs. Innovative methods of achieving this and of reaching that consumer have been frustrated by the outdated ethics of the professional institutions, although there are signs of a change in this direction. Lack of training in marketing skills remains a serious problem and little is being done to alleviate this at present. Professional arrogance and uncertainty will continue to inhibit the emergence of the marketing surveyor.

Residential practices are taking the lead, as Mann & Co and the Black Horse Agencies Group are showing. Both are market orientated, fully understanding that the consumer is paramount in their business development. Industrial and commercial practices have been very slow to realise this, although most claim that they have always been conscious of consumer need.

Nigel Stephens[1] warns of complacency at a time when other organisations could erode the residential estate agent's dominance of the market. The same warning applies to the commercial and industrial field — 1983 saw, for example, the continuing growth of ORC Relocation Consultants International, a successful property marketing group headquartered in Bristol.

Market forces are not recognised or acted upon quickly enough and the tremendous value of market research still fails to be recognised by the profession although, again, there are promising signs from such practices as Healey & Baker.

The RICS final year examination syllabus covers "marketing" inadequately and apart from including "management" under the same heading, does not yet include any marketing questions in the examination itself. This unhappy situation will not be resolved until those responsible commit sufficient resources to the problem.

A more detailed examination of what marketing is all about is given in Chapter 2. The basic definition of "identifying, anticipating and satisfying consumer needs at a profit" applies equally to the letting of property and to the provision of expert services by the professional practice. In fact, the definition applies to all who provide a product or a service for which a charge is made. Given that planning regulations continue to influence the location and type of developments, the profession has failed to recognise the impact of the new technology consumer on the property market.

Marketing is still confused with selling, but the surveyor should never misunderstand the relationship of these two terms. Selling is one method of communicating with a potential customer — there are others, such as advertising and mailshots. All these communicative activities come under the heading of "promotion", which is but one part of marketing. The practice should not underestimate the power of the new breed of surveyor salesmen — once he is properly trained.

The last few years have seen the emergence of strategic management and marketing planning as a new force in business. This market-led activity seeks to introduce a procedure for survival and growth in the ever-changing industrial and commercial environment. The property practice, too, can incorporate this dynamic management thinking into its future development, and a broad procedure is outlined in Chapter 2.

The state of the United Kingdom property market is discussed in Chapter 3, where difficulties are experienced in assessing take-up of premises. Data on stock are freely available from a number of

Summary and Conclusions 155

sources, but a need for better market research is necessary. Clearly, the amount of industrial floorspace available in January 1983 presents an overwhelming problem for the commercial agent chasing an ever-decreasing market about which he is badly informed. Explanation is given on the property consumer and how he is affected by the business environment.

Measurement of current and future demand is seen as a key issue in property dealing. Too much emphasis has been placed on historical data and anecdotal evidence. A difficult but essential area for the surveyor, demand estimation will be a vital weapon, and forecasting methods, developed by consumer companies, may have valuable applications in property development. The future looks bleak for 1984 and 1985, except perhaps in retail property. If high technology is one growth area, has the profession now got to grips with this field? Can the institutions be persuaded to invest in "high-tech" developments?

Chapter 4 discusses the property "product" in terms of premises, expert services and the practice itself. Some institutions are now questioning the ability of the commercial agent when it comes to professional investment advice, and relationships of long standing are in jeopardy as clients demand a more professional marketing-orientated service. Clearly, agents will have to display a better understanding of markets and show greater innovation if they are to convince clients that fees are justifiable or that promotional costs are effective. Fee arrangements could be reorganised to suit the client rather than following established institutional procedures.

Advice is given on how a buyer thinks and why companies buy or lease property. The "product life-cycle" concept, a major aspect of marketing, is also explained with hypotheses put forward on property product life-cycles.

In attempting to answer the question of slow reaction by the profession to the impact of high-technology industry, Chapter 4 offers a number of possible reasons. Traditional approaches to a non-traditional growth area are seen as the overall inhibiting factor.

It is now widely accepted that image and presentation as well as location are significant issues in property disposal. These are not the only aspects, however, and the key to successful sales is the recognition and ranking of those items that do affect the decision-making process undertaken by companies when it comes to premises. A more marketing-orientated approach is also needed when it comes to pricing. Maybe too much reliance is placed on historical and comparative methods rather than on a consumer-based analysis of what the market will actually pay for property or professional services.

Although not yet fully committed, the investing institutions seem ready to hear about new schemes that have real evidence of market demand, have been properly evaluated in competitive terms and include a budgeted promotional plan. Advice is given on how to prepare such a proposal.

Marketing the practice itself is considered to be as important as the firm's ability to sell property, and this is discussed in Chapter 5. Marketing the practice cannot be left to an advertising or public relations agency, and unless the practice has the marketing skills in-house it is unlikely to have the necessary trained staff to market itself effectively as a viable and efficient professional entity. Credibility with clients and potential customers is built on the firm's communicative ability and its understanding of the client's expectations of the practice.

The image of the commercial agent is not good and will continue to worsen as market conditions decline unless the practice makes deliberate plans to enhance its image in the market place. This can be done by the search for a competitive edge, which can be based on a number of facets currently available to the innovative practice. The establishment of an edge may be in the development of new services, staff-training in selling skills, fees and charges to clients or simply based upon an imaginative promotional campaign. An aggressive approach to new markets could put an agency ahead of its competitors.

Chapter 6 covers the raw material of marketing — market research. Even now in the property industry too much reliance is placed upon "gut-feel", or the developer's "nose", a dangerous practice in a depressed market. Market research is necessary to augment these traditional methods by providing reliable, objective "consumer" data. Seen for too long by the property profession as something to do with soap powder, market research is the reason that Texas Instruments and Barratt Homes are so successful.

In the United States the property industry is ahead in the use of consumer market research as an input to development appraisal, and such research is considered to be as vital as a soil-survey. Advice is given in Chapter 6 on the most applicable research techniques for the profession and on how to set up a research project for a proposed development scheme. The implications of market research for economic and development planning are significant, and the viability of schemes presented to investors would also be greatly enhanced if the proposals were market-research based.

The scale and complexity of today's property markets require a "rifle" rather than a "shotgun" approach to the marketing of commercial and industrial property. This new approach is called segmentation and targeting and is outlined in Chapter 7. Segmentation utilises market research to identify "buying groups" who share a common need. The technique also helps to establish and rank the purchase decision variables held by that group, or "target market". In order to be fruitful, however, the target market must be measurable, accessible and substantial.

A practice's ability to attack a target profitably will also depend upon its corporate objectives, its resources and, most importantly, the activities of its competitors. While a form of market segmentation analysis is practised by the United States property developer, certain basic assumptions, such as continuing employment growth, are proving to be unreliable. United Kingdom developers and their agents can easily avoid this obvious trap.

The plethora of communicative activities concerned with bringing the product to the customer are included in Chapter 8 under promotion. Promotion is not another word for advertising, neither is it a different term for marketing; all methods of communication with potential buyers are promotional activites, only the mix varies. The value of target market identification is that the promotional mix is determined by the market and not by the practice or its advisers.

Buyers of industrial and commercial property are seen as high information-seekers and often respond well to direct promotional techniques. Advertising agents support property advertising for obvious reasons; many agents depend upon it because they feel that they have no alternative. Following an explanation of what advertising is and how it works, guidance is given on how to make it more effective and how to brief and control an advertising agency.

The last five years have seen an increase in the use of other promotional techniques, most of which come under the heading of press and public relations, or PR for short. The property and national press has never been exploited by the chartered practice: much secrecy still abounds and good newsworthy stories tend to be clouded with vagueness — not surprisingly, since good newscopy can only really be prepared by journalists.

Under sales promotion, Chapter 8 discusses the relative value of mailshots, literature, site boards, exhibitions and so on. Literature is seen as an expensive item, and often too much thought is given to gimmickry and impact at the expense of the consumer. While the use of each activity depends upon the budget available and the innovative skills of the commercial agent, no single activity should be seen as generating sales in isolation. The strength of a promotional campaign lies in the integration of all methods in a balanced and sustained thrust.

A firm rationale is required for budgeting and monitoring

promotional spend. This must be based on what is required to do the job rather than on what the client feels is necessary. Budget allocations are very rarely based on a promotional plan and should properly reflect the needs of the target market and the resources of the client.

Failing to monitor the effectiveness of a promotional campaign is like running a business without bookkeeping. It is both efficient and sensible to measure results against spend and to be able to explain short-fall to a client. Effective targeting and a well-planned campaign that fully involves the client will help to substantiate results — whether good or bad. As much as possible must be done to avoid cost wastage, and at the end of the chapter further advice is given on how to save promotional money.

I consider selling to be so significant as an effective promotional function that Chapter 9 is entirely devoted to all aspects of the selling function. Despite the value of the salesman/surveyor, most practices seem reluctant to admit that this skill is at the core of their practice. Today's property market requires both professional salesmen and professionals who can sell. Both work as an integrated team in the market-orientated practice, where everyone is selling — from senior partner to receptionist.

The question of "hard-sell" or "soft-sell" is irrelevant because the need today is for the property salesman who recognises problems of clients and proposes profitable solutions. A balance of ages and experience can be an asset in a property team where many kinds of prospective buyers must be accommodated. Personality, appearance and technical knowledge are critical, as the tasks facing the salesman of the 1990s are new and challenging. The approach to the job can be creative and exciting, but full management support is essential.

Remuneration and incentives need to be realistic, bearing in mind the job that has to be done by the salesman in the depressed property market. Advice is also given on sales training and how to run a sales office with computer support.

Recent marketing developments

What has happened in property marketing in the last six months? Little has happened that fills me with optimism. I have looked in vain for a thrusting new direction by the professional societies and the commercial agent. Instead I see frustration, as many keep referring to the profession's inability to get the marketing philosophy on board. I see pessimism mixed with hopes of a financial recovery (even here experts disagree). I still meet commercial agents using "marketing" as another word for "selling", but not really understanding either, and I still read promotional schedules containing only

Summary and Conclusions

traditional proposals. Brave attempts by marketer Derrick Porter to offer sales advice to property developers via his advertisement in *Marketing* last September obviously came to naught, as he reported in December that response to his campaign had been "in the negative".

The Enterprise Business Park in the London Enterprise Zone was anounced in July 1983, with Tony Grant of Grant & Partners keen to emphasise the design requirements of the LDDC. The architects have designed "unusual and flexible" buildings amounting to 90,000 sq ft which are "intended for science-based industry and high-office-content commercial users[2]. This familiar statement is repeated on the very same page of *Chartered Surveyor Weekly*, where the Northern England Development Association announced a £100m project for Preston. The development proposes provision for "high-technology industry" and a "40-acre business park". No mention is made in either article of the background to these proposals. Has market research been used to identify a need? How do the letting agents intend to approach the target market? Has the effect of competitive schemes been taken into account? How big is the potential market? What price will the target market pay for these units? Has the competitive edge been established for these schemes?

Derek Penfold is pessimistic in his excellent prologue to the 1983 *Estates Gazette* Property Market Review[3]. Referring to property prospects of 1983 as showing little improvement, he says: "Would the market learn from 1982 and apply its knowledge, rather than compound errors? Sadly, there was little sign of innovation or constructive effort in many spheres." Further on he specifically mentions marketing and makes a valid comparison with American real estate practice. "In the United Kingdom the nominally-abolished fee scales do little to encourage more than a flash of brilliance, and the advertising and marketing talents so evident in selling consumer products are only rarely employed in property."

Despite this, there has been some innovation, if only in advertising copy. For example, plates 37 to 42 show more creative use of colour and a tendency towards clever terminology.
creative use of colour and a tendency towards clever terminology.

In the same issue of *Estates Gazette*[3] Andrew Huntley of Richard Ellis described the trend in 1983 as "occupier-led", forcing the institutions to reappraise their investment expectations from commercial property. And he makes a significant observation that shows the unfocused approach still being made by developers: "Over the recession years, there was surprisingly little let-up in new construction and development and as a consequence over the last two years supply has far outstripped demand in many sectors of the property market". Is it any wonder that John Plender said in December that there was too little forecasting in the property market and that investment was "certainly about to go into decline"? He also accused fund managers of being short on entrepreneurialism.

High technology has been discussed a lot in this book and throughout the year in the profession, yet are we any nearer understanding the complexity of this area and its impact upon property? Nicholas Owen of Herring Son & Daw[3] quite rightly accuses the industry of "self-defeating abandon" by labelling ordinary industrial estates as high-technology parks. This simply will not fool any high-technology company, especially one originating from the United States. Herring Son & Daw's market research points to the "coalescence of the work process, so that office, laboratory, production and sales activities go forward alongside one another in ever-varying proportions". Nicholas Owen seems to be aware of the value of research as a design input in that he describes the high-technology property as "a concept far removed from traditional industrial buildings". I applaud the consumer-led approach being taken by Nicholas Owen and his colleagues in Herring Son & Daw: one wonders if such input has been available to the two schemes mentioned earlier.

The King & Co[4] report states that at December 1983 171.6m sq ft of industrial floorspace stood empty, an increase of 65m sq ft, or 38%, since I started writing this book, although there are indications that the rate of increase — having been a frightening 40% pa — is slowing down. Offices have been in some demand in 1983 in London but nowhere else in the country, except Scotland, which is reported to be more active than at any time in the previous five years[3]. The only really productive sector has been in the retail trade, where, according to Harvey Spack of Harvey Spack Field, the retail market is "currently in a very buoyant mood[3]." This appears to be due to better takings by the retailers rather than to aggressive and innovative marketing by commercial agents.

Residential property had an interesting year and, while this does not involve this book directly, some observations are pertinent. I was intrigued by an advertisement for a three-day study course endorsed by the RICS that was held in Oxford last April. The speakers came from reputable chartered practices and the subject of the first day was marketing. The advertisement asks if marketing is "The expensive luxury or the vital influence? Is it all a waste of money? Do you really need an expert?" Ironically, the presentation on the third day was by Roy Mercer of Black Horse Agencies, now top of the league with 104 offices and nearly 1,000 staff. Roy Mercer's views on consumer marketing are clear from his article in the *Estates Gazette*

Property Review. He states: "Increasingly it is apparent that this is a 'people' business and that the marketing and presentation of property needs to be handled with feeling and flexibility by well-trained people who are dedicated and can communicate. However, the training of those handling the client seems to have been very much a Cinderella area in the past and public opinion proves that." So it has been with most aspects of marketing.

While on residential agency practice, it is interesting to see Jackson Property Services, whom I have mentioned earlier in this book, now standing at number 34 in the league with 15 offices, 200 staff and not one chartered surveyor.

Barratts continue to make money from applied marketing. An article in the US publication *Business Week* in July 1983 relates their activities in California[5]. Referring to their success in the United States, the article maintains that Barratts revolutionised the industry by breaking the market down into "different purchasing groups", segmenting it and clearly identifying the "specific needs of each group". Nothing more than a straightforward application of marketing techniques. Is it so "revolutionary"?

Unfortunately the property industry is not the only industry still behind the times in the adoption of marketing. The marketing director of Sodastream, Harry Hemens, writing in an article in a recent copy of *Marketing*[6], deplores the fact that an astonishing proportion of our larger companies still do not have a marketing director. He says: "Twenty years ago I was prepared to accept that many people felt that marketing was just a sophisticated word for selling. Nowadays my tolerance is not so high. Why is there so little understanding of this vital aspect of commercial life?"

The future

So, where do we now stand? It seems that there is much to be done, but at least some property professionals are starting to do it; others are still confused and some, no doubt, are bemused by the advice I offer in this book. Derek Penfold refers to marketing in his prologue[3] as "one area of professional practice where debate has at last got under way, though very gently". He advises that for 1984 the challenge will be for agents and developers to "treat that all-important group — the tenants — with far more intelligence and consideration".

In the same 1983 review, Paul Bewers of Peter Taylor & Co talks about design as now a crucial factor in any speculative development. "Tenants are not prepared to accept poor quality, and many schemes which fall short of what is required will remain unlet for some time," he says. A bad situation for all, yet one that can be avoided by a serious application of marketing principles. Paul Bewers observes, however, "a noticeable change of attitude by developers and investors, who are now much more sensitive to providing buildings of quality and identity that are in line with the tenant's requirements". Could this be light at the end of the tunnel of frustration? Could developers, investors and agents actually be heeding the needs of the consumer?

I am also encouraged to see research playing more of a role in the property profession. Several agents, including Herring Son & Daw and Debenham Tewson & Chinnocks, have published good research findings. The article by Russell Schiller of Hillier, Parker May & Rowden in the *Estates Gazette* Property Review[3] was, however, disappointing. There seems to be some confusion about the market in the article. The writer is quite correct in advocating that research data is an aid to decision-making and reduces risk, but the size of the market cannot be determined by an analysis of "the amount of money held and invested and the amount of floorspace available for letting". This surely is an assessment of stock — not market size. Russell Schiller does refer to the availability of government statistics (again on stock levels) and to specialist agencies who "have been set up to supply the need". The one quoted is JICTAR, a TV audience measurement panel, which seems a bit irrelevant in the article.

The real crux of market research, which the article does not refer to, although the words "market" and "research" appear in different contexts, eventually appears in the third column. Referring to the shortcomings of using historical data to forecast trends, the writer says: "One of the better ways around this problem [of forecasting] is to study the needs of users of property". Here we have the whole rationale of market research and Russell Schiller mentions recent research reports that I have referred to on a number of occasions. After making what is to a marketer an obvious statement — "as demand for property remains fairly weak, the study of tenants' needs is likely to become more important" — the writer makes a valid point on another benefit of research to the chartered practice, which was mentioned in Chapter 4. He states: "Many institutional investors look to research material to justify their decisions to their trustees" — an activity likely to increase if property remains unlet for a long time.

Clearly, some agents are beginning to realise the various benefits of marketing, including research, that can be obtained with relative ease.

Some experts now feel that the industrial property market is beginning to recover and that growth in that market can be expected, but there is real concern by tenants about operating costs and capability, image and identity and quality of design. The market will change again and the property profession must be ready next time. The *United States Industrial Development Handbook*[7] states that three areas of technological change can be expected to induce new trends — transportation, materials handling and communications. This change and its implications must be identified and anticipated if we are to avoid the current confusion that exists between consumer, developer, investor and agent.

Enormous problems also exist for the agent who has instructions to dispose of second-hand premises — both factories and offices — many of which are unsuitable and unwanted. London agents should not be complacent, because although current demand may appear to be buoyant in the South-East concentration of effort brings problems and competition for the attention of every potential buyer. Many commercial agents may fail to survive the next few years without a major change in their business practice. The writing is on the wall now. Even the National Association of Estates Agents regard marketing and computerisation as two revolutions that will affect the whole of their industry.

The future of the industrial and commercial property market inextricably involves the surveyor and valuer. It is up to him as the professional expert to research the market, forecast demand, guide developers, persuade institutions and let the properties. In essence the surveyor and the marketer are one and the same.

A final quote from the *United States Industrial Development Handbook*. "Perhaps no other aspect of the business of buying, improving and selling industrial property has changed as dramatically over the past decade as marketing techniques. Until recently the business was conducted by a number of professionals who relied upon their intuition and experience to identify product demand and to market property. This informal approach will be supplanted by totally different tactics." Will you be ready?

Chapter 10. References.

[1] "The Practice of Estate Agency" Nigel Stephens. The Estates Gazette Ltd, 1980.
[2] Property News. *Chartered Surveyor Weekly, 21 July 1983.*
[3] *1983 Property Market Review. Estates Gazette,* January 21 1984.
[4] Industrial Floorspace Survey, 1983. King & Co.
[5] "International Business". *Business Week*, July 18 1983.
[6] Perspective. Harry Hemens. *Marketing*, January 5 1984.
[7] *United States Industrial Development Handbook* 1980. Urban Land Institute.

Index

A

Advertising 4, 16, 45, 51, 73, 74, 76, 79, 86, 90, 92, 95, 103, 104, 107, 109, 110, 111, 112, 113, 114, 115, 116, 118, 119, 120, 125, 126, 128, 129, 130, 133, 134, 141, 154, 156, 157, 159, 160
Advertising Agency 24, 113, 114, 117, 127, 149, 157
African States 33
Agricultural Market 21
AIDA 139
Allen & Harris 151
American economists 76
American real estate 67
Apple Computers 150
Architects 38, 49, 59, 82, 159
Audio-visual 104
Aztec West 85, 96

B

Barratt 3, 62, 90, 91, 134, 156, 161
Bewers, Paul 162
Birmingham 29
Black Horse Agency 4, 21, 40, 62, 75, 153, 161
Boston Consulting Group 19
brand loyalty 73
British Petroleum 110

C

Cadbury 111
CALUS 58, 90, 103, 134
Cambridge Science Park 55, 85, 96
channels of persuasion 16
Chartered Surveyor Weekly 112, 113
College of Estate Management 5
Colorado 82
Commercial Union 96
Commissions 68, 72, 135, 146, 147
Commodore 150
Competitive edge 22, 24, 65, 67, 68, 69, 70, 72
Competitive parity-system 128
Competitive position 31, 60, 94
Computer 70, 80, 150, 151, 152, 158
Confederation of British Industry 2
Consumers Association 64
Consumerism 1, 31
Corporate identity 72
Crest 99
Cripps, Peter 140

D

Debenham Tewson & Chinnocks 162
Dek 150
demand 31, 33, 34, 35, 36, 38, 39, 40, 41, 44, 46, 48,
 .... 49, 60, 79, 86, 89, 90, 94, 100, 101, 139, 156, 163, 164
demand, consumer 1, 32, 33, 34, 57, 58
demand, current 36, 37, 66, 155
demand, future 33, 37, 66, 155
demand, property 33
Department of Environment (DOE) 28, 30
Developer 31, 33, 34, 35, 40, 49, 58, 59, 60, 76,
 .... 82, 84, 85, 86, 87, 98, 99, 100, 101, 109, 117, 118, 119, 127,
 .... 129, 134, 157, 159, 160, 162
Digital 150
Dragon 150

E

Estates Times 112, 113
Europe 33, 110, 114
European Society of Marketing Research 10
Exhibitions 74, 104, 107, 109, 124, 125, 126

F

Fees	46, 48, 64, 72, 91, 160
Fieldwork	88, 91, 94
Film	104, 124
Financial Times	110, 117
Ford, Henry	14
Forecast/ing	18, 22, 38, 39, 40, 100, 163, 164

G

gap analysis	97
General Electric Company	21
GLC	29
Grant & Partners	159
Greenbury, Stephen	85

H

Harvard Business School	138
Healey & Baker	40, 154
Heath, Edward	32
Hemens, Harry	161
Herman Miller	34
Herring Son & Daw	162
high-technology	15, 36, 37, 41, 42, 44, 48, 55, 56, 59, 85, 87, 96, 122, 155, 159, 160
Holborn, borough of	29
Honda motorcycles	14
Honeywell	150

I

IBM	150
ICFC	70
ICL	150
image building	72
Imperial Chemical Industries	2
Incorporated Society of Valuers and Auctioneers	4, 5, 13, 72, 75, 141, 151
industrial floorspace	27, 28, 39, 98, 155, 160
Industrial Marketing Research Association	10, 92
Institute of Directors	125
Institute of Marketing	9, 10, 13, 68, 148

J

Jackson Property Services 149, 161
Journalists 109, 116, 117

K

Korea 32

L

Leighton Goldhill 151
Life-cycles 48, 49, 51, 100, 155
Linford Wood 56
Literature 45, 69, 104, 107, 117, 120, 121,
.... 122, 130, 142, 143, 158, 159
Lloyds Bank 23, 40
London 28, 29, 30, 161, 163
London Enterprise Zone 159

M

Mailshots 16, 46, 47, 75, 104, 109, 119, 120, 154
Management Consultant 45
Mann & Co. 4, 74, 153
Market
    – analysis 6, 7, 101
    – "build-up" method 37
    – demand 7, 34
    – forces 117, 139, 154
    – gap 14, 31, 36, 65, 79, 101
    – growth 114
    – knowledge 66
    – orientation 3, 4, 7
    – place 33, 72, 79, 156
    – potential 23, 36, 37, 86, 99
    – projections 84
    – requirements 15
    – research 6, 8, 10, 24, 32, 38, 44, 47, 49, 55,
      .... 60, 66, 76, 97, 98, 106, 107, 136, 140, 141, 154,
      .... 155, 156, 157, 159, 160, 163
    – segment 36, 101
    – share 19, 23, 35, 37, 86, 97, 109, 128
    – size 36
    – value 57
    – viability 66, 96
Market Location Ltd 151
Market Research Society 10, 92

Index

Marketing
- campaign 44, 45
- Diploma 9
- function 5, 18
- information 33, 57, 79, 80, 84, 87
- Institute of 9, 10, 13, 68, 148
- magazine 9
- mix 25, 56, 76, 100, 103, 118
- model 90
- opportunities 21, 22, 79, 97, 100
- plan 22, 25, 56
- planning 18, 19, 21, 22, 56, 101
- policy 7, 18
- strategy 15, 25, 100
- surveyor 9, 11
- system 24
- team 23
- techniques 6, 8, 12
Media 66, 74
Mercator Computer Systems 151
Mercer, Roy 161
McGraw Hill 111, 127
Microscope 151
Milton Keynes Development Corporation 56
Monopolies Commission 3, 62, 64
Morton-Smith, Guy 85
Motorola 150
Multiple Agency 46

N

National Association of Estate Agents 151, 164
New Homes Marketing Board 65
Newton, Derek 138
Northern England Development Corporation 159

O

Office 29, 30, 39, 49, 59, 84, 95, 161
- space 29, 34, 58
Olivetti 150
Orchard-Lisle, Paul 40, 85
ORC Relocation International Ltd 154
Osborne, Charles 151

P

Peter Taylor & Co. 162
planning 82
    – authority 34
    – policy 34
    – regulations 34
Plender, John 160
Porter, Derrick 159
pound contribution method 128
preference segments 98
press 73, 74, 90, 104, 107, 109, 110,
.... 111, 115, 116, 117, 118, 119, 130
Preston 159
pricing 24, 45, 56, 57, 58, 60, 66, 72, 86, 88, 90, 92, 140
product
    – knowledge 66
    – orientation 2, 4, 34
promotion 4, 37, 44, 72, 86, 90, 103, 104, 110, 113,
.... 118, 119, 120, 124, 126, 127, 128, 133, 148, 154, 157
property
    – management 47
    – market 22, 27, 29, 30, 35, 40
    – press 45, 59, 73
Property Agents Computer Team 151
Property Research Team 92

Q

Quantity Surveyors 49

R

radio 104
rating 47, 70
Rent Acts 34
retail 84, 94
    – development 15
    – growth 41
    – premises 30, 69
    – property market 30, 31
    – space 31
Retail Audits Ltd. 92
Retail Price Index 110
Richard Ellis 151
Royal Institution of Chartered Surveyors 4, 5, 11, 13, 25, 63,
.... 72, 75, 86, 134, 141, 151, 154, 161
Rushton, J. E. 135, 148

S

Sales 22, 33, 34, 36, 39, 69, 74, 86, 110,
.... 111, 112, 116, 118, 123, 128, 130
- analysis 86
- brochures 101
- force 16, 38, 66, 103, 106, 115
- forecasting 21, 33
- man 18, 38, 62, 65, 67, 104, 120, 124, 125, 126, 127, 158
- office 69, 75, 158
- operation 62
- organisation 15
- promotion 24, 114, 119, 124, 126, 127
- staff 70, 75, 76
- team 47, 51, 68, 109
- training 70, 158
Saudi Arabia 23
Scotland 161
segment/ation 22, 24, 35, 48, 76, 157
selling 4, 15, 16, 64, 68, 103, 104, 110, 116, 154, 156, 158, 162
signboards 104, 107, 123, 124
Sinclair 80, 150
Sirius Computers 150
site boards 72
sole agency 46
south-east 30, 75, 163
sponsorship 74, 104, 115, 118
staff recruitment 70
Standard Industrial Classification (SIC) 37
statistical-demand analysis 39
Stovold, Colin 75
structural surveys 47, 70
Sun Alliance 56, 96

T

Taiwan 32
task method 114, 127, 128
Televideo 150
Television 104, 110
territorial potential 36
test-market method 38
Texas Instruments 18, 156
Time magazine 113
Time-series analysis 39
Tweddle, J. V 85

U

Ultra-Brite 99
United Kingdom 9, 11, 79, 83, 91, 95, 97, 101, 110,
............111, 112, 116, 120, 124, 125, 139, 148, 153, 154, 157, 160
United States 33, 34, 35, 56, 58, 59, 62, 73, 82, 83, 86,
..................101, 110, 111, 112, 113, 124, 150, 156, 157, 160, 161

W

West Midlands 117
"Which?" 64
Wimpey 62
word-processor 150